Cambridge Papers in Sociology No. 3

PERCEPTIONS OF WORK

Cambridge Studies in Sociology

1 *The Affluent Worker: Industrial Attitudes and Behaviour* by John H. Goldthorpe, David Lockwood, Frank Bechhofer and Jennifer Platt.

2 *The Affluent Worker: Political Attitudes and Behaviour* by John H. Goldthorpe, David Lockwood, Frank Bechhofer and Jennifer Platt.

3 *The Affluent Worker in the Class Structure* by John H. Goldthorpe, David Lockwood, Frank Bechhofer and Jennifer Platt.

4 *Men in Mid-Career: A Study of British Managers and Technical Specialists* by Cyril Sofer.

5 *Family Structure in Nineteenth Century Lancashire* by Michael Anderson.

Cambridge Papers in Sociology

1 *Size of Industrial Organization and Worker Behaviour* by Geoffrey K. Ingham.

2 *Workers' Attitudes and Technology* by Dorothy Wedderburn and Rosemary Crompton.

3 *Perceptions of Work* by H. Beynon and R. M. Blackburn.

Perceptions of Work

Variations within a Factory

by H. BEYNON
Lecturer in Sociology, University of Bristol

and R. M. BLACKBURN
Senior Research Officer, Department of Applied Economics, University of Cambridge

CAMBRIDGE
AT THE UNIVERSITY PRESS
1972

Published by the Syndics of the Cambridge University Press
Bentley House, 200 Euston Road, London NW1 2DB
American Branch: 32 East 57th Street, New York, N.Y. 10022

© Cambridge University Press 1972

Library of Congress Catalogue Card Number: 72-80594

ISBNs: 0 521 07384 7 *hard covers*
       0 521 09727 4 *paperback*

Printed in Great Britain by
W. Heffer & Sons Ltd., Cambridge

Contents

Preface   vii

1   INTRODUCTION   1
    The study of work   1
    The approach   6

2   THE WORKERS AT BROMPTON   13
    Technology, work and wages   15
    Social characteristics of the workforce   23
    The trade union   33
    Summary   35

3   THE WORKER AND THE FIRM   39
    Finding work   39
    Assessment of the firm   45
    Perceptions of management   55
    Summary   59

4   THE WORKER AND HIS JOB   61
    Important aspects of a job   61
    Expectations and satisfaction   63
    Doing the job   72
    Friendships at work   80
    Payment system   82
    Summary   84

5   THE WORKER AND SUPERVISION   88
    Workers' views about being a supervisor   88
    The supervisors   94
    Summary   105

6   WORKER REPRESENTATION   107
    Grievances   108
    The workers and the trade union   113
    The shop-stewards   128

	Joint consultation	136
	Summary	140
7	CONCLUSIONS	144
	Living with work	145
	Some implications for the study of work	153
	Appendix: THE INTERVIEW SCHEDULE	162
	References	169
	Index	173

Preface

The research on which this report is based was carried out at the request of William Gourmet & Sons, who gave us complete freedom to carry out the research as we thought fit. They in no way influenced the way in which we conducted our investigations or the writing of this report. The firm, however, wish to remain anonymous, and Gourmets is not their proper name. The fieldwork was carried out during 1966 by Huw Beynon. Both authors shared in the design, analysis and writing up of results. We should like to express our thanks to the people who made this study possible: the management, the union and above all the workers who had quite enough problems of their own without answering our innumerable questions. We are also indebted to many colleagues who have taken an interest in the work. In particular we should like to mention J. A. Banks, J. M. Mann, T. Nichols, K. Prandy and A. Stewart. However, they are not to blame for what follows.

1 Introduction

This is a study of the ways in which workers relate, and adapt to their work situation. It is set in a single factory, so that those aspects of the situation relating to the particular employer, such as the firm's profitability, size and reputation are the same for all the workers. It also follows that, in a general sense, the workers are in a common labour market.[1] However, this still leaves considerable variation in their experience of work. On the one hand this is influenced by the work group and the specific conditions relating to the worker's particular job; on the other hand it depends on the values and expectations which each worker brings to the work situation. The aim of this study is to examine the relationship of these two influences in determining variations in perceptions of work. It is argued that the organisational structure and the social characteristics of the men and women employed in the factory combine to produce four relatively distinct groups within the workforce which tend to evaluate their position in different ways. The presentation of the study is primarily descriptive, seeking to illustrate the patterns of orientation and perception, but at the same time this has a theoretical purpose. It may be seen as a contribution to the current discussion of the nature and consequence of worker involvement, as well as assisting our understanding of the social forces that operate within a local labour market.

THE STUDY OF WORK

Few things exert a greater influence upon people's lives than the work they do. The study of work has been the specific concern of industrial sociologists during this century yet few of their studies have succeeded in grasping the full impact that work exerts within our society. There are many reasons for this, the most obvious being the rather strong association of classical industrial sociology with the aims and interests of management.

While the human relations approach corrected some of the cruder behaviourist assumptions of the scientific management theorists it shared

---

1 The relevance of these common features, however, may vary for different workers, since their effect is largely mediated by personnel policy which may discriminate between categories of workers, as for instance men and women. Furthermore — a related point — within a local labour market, the position of different types of workers varies appreciably. These points are considered in greater detail in later chapters.

with them the assumption that conflicts of interest were not structured into the work situation. This approach highlighted the significance of social relationships within the factory and the operation of group norms. In the managerial approach which stemmed from this the key to productivity was seen to lie in happy integrated groups. Worker satisfaction was seen as determined by styles of supervisory leadership, participation, consultation and the formation of cohesive work groups. A consequence of these foci of interest was that the analysis began and ended at the factory gates.

Against this there has emerged an approach which has emphasised the fundamental importance of technological variables upon the nature of work and work place behaviour. In Britain this approach has been exemplified by the work at the Tavistock Institute and the Department of Social Science at Liverpool, and has received its most positive statement in the work of Joan Woodward.[2]

The technical implications approach sees the technological structure of the work process imposing itself upon the objective structure of work relations. The structure of work groups, together with the structure of management, is seen to vary with the technological requirements of the productive process. As such this position served as an antidote to the simple ideas of the earlier managerial theories. Also, these theorists have to some extent helped to focus attention upon the nature of inter-group conflict within the factory, which the earlier schools ignored. To this extent, therefore, the technical implications approach was an important step forward. Nevertheless it has retained an essentially closed institutional framework and so has not freed the study of work from the confines of the factory. It has brought to the fore a major influence on worker behaviour, but it does not provide a complete basis of explanation. The actions of men are not a determined reaction to the machine structure of their work environment; rather they reflect the interpretation and attempts to control this environment.[3] Gouldner has argued on this point that the worker brings to the job situation a whole series of 'latent roles' relating to age, sex, ethnic origin, religion, class background, etc., which he can call upon to interpret that situation. Thus, he claims an adequate consideration of the nature of worker

---

2 See particularly J. Woodward, *Industrial Organisations*. For reviews of the Liverpool and Tavistock work, see R. K. Brown 'Participation, Conflict and Change in Industry' and R. K. Brown, 'Research and Consultancy in Industrial Enterprises'.
3 A notable example of workers' attempts to control is 'working back' on the automobile assembly line, as reported by G. R. Walker and R. H. Guest, *The Man or the Assembly Line*.

involvement in a factory will need to venture beyond the enterprise as its unit of study.[4]

This attempt to release the study of worker involvement from the restrictions of a determinate organisational structure unites a group of theorists into what can be broadly termed the 'action approach'. Such an approach starts from the principle that if people define situations as real, they are real in their consequences.[5] Thus, in what is perhaps the best known British application of this approach, the authors advocate using 'a frame of reference within which the actors' own definitions of the situations in which they are engaged are taken as an initial basis for the explanation of their social behaviour and relationships . . . (which) would direct attention systematically to the *variety of meanings* which work may come to have for industrial employees'.[6]

This approach differs importantly from those discussed earlier in that it offers the possibility of treating the worker as a whole person. Instead of the fragmented study of the worker who exists only in relation to the work situation, it takes account of the worker's life beyond the factory gates and the relevance of this for work.

Within such an approach technology does not cease to be important, it merely takes on a different significance. The extent of the influence of technology upon the ideas of workers, for example, cannot be directly deduced from the physical fact of the machinery, but from the interpretation of the machinery by the actors in the work situation. Consequently it is clear that a consideration of workers' orientations will be useful as a basis for explaining variations in workplace behaviour. It is quite surprising, for example, that although there has been quite a detailed consideration given by sociologists to the problem of 'why do married women work', and 'How do school leavers choose their first job?' there has been little or no discussion of how these groups react to, and affect the factories in which they work. Viewed in this way the consideration of orientations is similar to that of 'latent social identities' referred to by Gouldner.[7]

The notion of an orientation to work is also important for an understanding of the operation of a labour market and the study of occupational choice. Workers will tend, as far as possible, to select

---

4 A. W. Gouldner, 'Organisational Analysis'.
5 The principle was formulated in W. l. and D. S. Thomas, *The Child in America*, though it was entailed in much of the earlier work of W. I. Thomas; see, for example, *The Unadjusted Girl.*
6 J. H. Goldthorpe *et al., The Affluent Worker: Industrial Attitudes and Behaviour*, p. 184.
7 A. W. Gouldner, 'Organisational Analysis'.

employment in keeping with their priorities in what they want from work. This, we might expect, would bring together workers with similar expectations into similar work situations. However, such self-selection is limited by lack of information about different jobs and, more basically, lack of opportunity. Even in full-employment the range of available jobs may be very restricted, and it cannot be assumed workers will obtain jobs which satisfy their most important expectations and desires. For instance, if the 'thesis of growing privatisation' presented by Goldthorpe and his colleagues is correct, we may expect many instrumentally orientated workers to be unable to obtain highly paid jobs and so work in quite different situations, where we suggest their perceptions and behaviour would also be quite different.

This brings us to a fundamental point. The way in which work is experienced depends neither on work factors nor orientation alone, but on the interaction of the two. Furthermore, an orientation to work should not be thought of as arising outside and brought into the work situation but as something which derives from the individual's total experience. In moving outside the factory gate we should beware of creating a false dichotomy between work and non-work life. The rejection of the adequacy of explanations based on technological determinacy and systems needs should not lead us to adopt one which replaces an analysis of the work situation with one based on prior orientations. We do not wish to imply that non-work factors are not of considerable importance. On the contrary, one of the basic propositions of this study is that orientations to work are related to structural features of the workers' biographies within which family position plays an important part. Thus, for instance, we would expect work to have a markedly different significance for young unmarried workers and those with two or three dependent children. Similarly we would expect that role segregation within the family would affect the significance attributed to work by male and female members of the family. However, the workers' biographies also include their experience of work and the labour market, which imposes an awareness of the limited possibilities open to them. At a point of time the way in which work is experienced is a complex evaluation of the various objective features of the particular work situation, which is based upon these orientations.

Within the work situation management are in a position of power from which they exercise a control which may well be in conflict with the worker's wants and expectations. As Gouldner points out, severe constraints are placed upon the aspects of his 'self' that the worker is able to demonstrate while at work.[8] It would be difficult, for example, for the assembly line worker in a

---

8 A. W. Gouldner, 'The Unemployed Self'.

car plant to display elements of creativity in his job without breaking the rules. Now while it is obviously possible for workers to choose such 'unrewarding' work, i.e. to sell large parts of their 'selves' for eight or nine hours a day, it does not necessarily follow that they will obtain what they consider to be adequate economic recompense.

It is only at the manual levels of the occupational hierarchy that people may have to sacrifice all other potential sources of satisfaction in order to gain significant economic rewards. Managers, for instance, usually have more rewarding work on all aspects, including pay. For this reason it is particularly useful to typify manual worker orientations according to the dominant aspect, as with the 'instrumental' orientations described by Goldthorpe et al.[9] We should not, however, let this lead us into overlooking the fact that workers, if given the opportunity, would welcome more satisfying rewards in other aspects of their work. This raises the point that the experience of workers is dependant upon their position within the class structure of society. Workers exercise very little control over many decisions which affect their lives. In this sense their position can be seen as one which embodies alienation.

On the other hand we should not overstate the limits on the worker's freedom. Collective action provides a basis to exercise some control over decisions taken at work and also in the wider society. Furthermore, within the work situation a worker's actions may be severely constrained, but the constraints vary in their intensity and can never become total. The expression of such freedom as the worker has is derived from his 'latent roles' − the total 'self' he brings to the work situation, which cannot be completely moulded by the forces that operate in that situation.

This leads us to a further point, concerning the social context of work activity. The workers themselves create this context and thus, in spite of limiting features of the technical and organisational structure, they exercise some control. This may be seen in the operation of group norms, as shown in many studies of the human relations school, but there is a further sense in which the social context is importantly outside management control. The attitudes of the individual workers, as well as the degree of group cohesion and collective organisation, are variables which together constitute the social context is which they spend their working lives. Perhaps we can demonstrate our point best by returning to our earlier example of work orientations being related to position within the family. We would expect the orientations toward work of an adolescent girl school-leaver to differ dramatically from

---

9 J. H. Goldthorpe et al., The Affluent Worker: Industrial Attitudes and Behaviour.

those of a forty-year-old married man with three children and a history of unemployment. When we examine their behaviour at work however, we would also expect that the adolescent girl would express her 'self' in a situation full of other adolescent girls rather differently from one dominated by middle-aged men. There would be further differences depending on whether or not the workers had established significant social relations or had organised themselves within a trade union.

This brief discussion has given the theoretical background to our study. We have used the concept of orientation to refer in a general way to a central organising principle which underlies people's attempts to make sense of their lives. We start from the belief that people's understanding of their work is important, and such understanding is significantly affected by their experience of work and is also related in some way to their understanding of other aspects of their lives. Furthermore it should not be considered independent of other people's interpretations and hence actions. People came to some accommodation with the limitations imposed by compliance in the world of work, but because of the stresses due to these limitations the accommodation is unlikely to be an easy one.

From this standpoint it follows that an analysis of worker behaviour must take account of the technical and social aspects of the situations in which the workers are located and the associated extrinsic rewards. However, to explain the variations in perceptions of work from which the behaviour derives, it is clearly necessary to study orientations to the different aspects of their work which are held by various sections of a labour force. It is also important to examine the extent to which expectations which derive from these orientations come into conflict with the expectations of the institutionalised holders of power within the work situation.

THE APPROACH

The research comprised a case study in a single factory. Much consideration has been given to the merits of the case study as a basis for sociological research,[10] and it is generally argued that if the research aims at developing valid generalisations it must be based upon a comparative analysis. But it does not follow that the interesting comparisons are between firms and not between sections of one firm. Clearly it depends on the objectives of the research. An hypothesis can be tested in one situation, but a comparative approach gives a greater range on variables for testing or theory development.

---

10 For a discussion of these arguments see the methodological appendix of S. M. Lipset *et al., Union Democracy.*

Ideally an investigation of a fully elaborated theoretical model should be comparative both within and between fully distinct employment situations. Our aim in this study, however, was much more limited. We were interested in examining tentatively the nature of the relationship between orientations to work and objective features of the work situation as it influenced perceptions of that situation. We felt that this could best be accomplished by an intensive investigation of a particular case. This approach had further attractions in that it would allow us to exercise some control over the objective structure of the work situation. By studying workers employed by the same firm, and thereby subject to the same basic conditions of employment, work rules and the like, working within a similar technological environment we would be able to examine variations in their subjective interpretations of the situation. This reasoning led us to base the research upon the labour force of a single factory. The case we chose was particularly attractive. The firm employed both men and women, the men being divided between permanent day and night shifts and the women between those who worked full-time and part-time.

In the first place we were approached by the company with a view to conducting an attitude survey of their employees. In discussions with senior management it was readily agreed that we should conduct the research in our own way and publish our findings. We then obtained the cooperation of the union, including approval of the research and access to all branch and shop-stewards' committee meetings. We were then in a position to commence the research although we still had to obtain the co-operation of the workers themselves.

The first few weeks of field work were spent walking around each of the departments talking to workers, shop-stewards and supervisors. As there was a tendency for the workers to define anyone not tied to a job on the belts as one of 'them', all conversations with the workers commenced, with the assistance of the shop-steward,[11] during tea breaks or in canteens and were continued in the job situation. During these observations and conversations we were trying to get some general idea of the ways in which the workers and the supervision comprehended work in the factory. At the same time we were building up an idea of the physical layout of the plant and the processes of interaction that took place between workers, both in their work situation and also during their tea and dinner breaks.

---

11 For an interesting discussion of the usefulness of personal contacts in observational research see the methodological appendix of W. F. Whyte, *Street Corner Society*.

This type of 'participant as observer'[12] approach was used throughout the study and provided us with a great amount of useful qualitative information. It was particularly useful in the early stages of the research when we were in the process of developing a number of hypotheses around which we were to base the research. These hypotheses were examined in greater detail in a series of formal interviews with workers. The flexibility afforded us by the observational approach was then of further use in that it enabled us to develop ideas that were suggested to us by responses in these interviews, and also to incorporate quickly into our research an examination of any issues or events which took place during the time we were at the plant.[13]

We have based the bulk of the evidence for the arguments we develop in this paper upon the data obtained from the responses to a structured interview schedule.[14] All these interviews were conducted in private in rooms away from the shop floor. They each took approximately forty-five minutes and were built around questions that had been pre-tested and found to yield relevant, reliable information. As all the interviews were carried out by one of the authors it was impossible to obtain an assessment of the extent to which he biased the information obtained, but any such interviewer bias tended to be constant throughout the sample. We were aware, however, that over the time we were in the factory the interviewer's orientation toward the research problem, and the attitudes held by the workers would be subject to change. In order to exert some control over these potential changes the interviewing was staggered into a number of stages. In each stage a percentage of the respondents in each stratum of the sample were interviewed, thus enabling us to attach greater validity to any observed differences between the strata.

---

12 R. L. Gold, 'Roles in Sociological Field Observations', p. 217, has pointed out that 'although basically similar to the complete observer role, the participant as observer role differs significantly in that both field worker and informant are aware that theirs is a field relationship. This mutual awareness tends to minimise problems of role pretending; yet, the role carries with it numerous opportunities for compartmentalising mistakes and dilemmas which typically bedevil the complete participant'. While this is so, however, the 'participant as observer' approach brings with it the important problem of role definition, i.e. how the actors in the social situation cope with the researcher, and vice versa.
13 These observations were also important in themselves, as they allowed us to check that responses given in the interview situation were a guide to action in the work situation. See I. Deutscher, 'Words and Deeds'. This type of approach has been used with a greater degree of formality and with considerable success by J. Kolaja in his study of *A Polish Factory*.
14 The interview schedule is reproduced in the Appendix.

8

We commenced our programme of formal interviewing during our fourth week at the factory. By this time we had discussed the project with representatives of all grades of management, including a large number of supervisors, and most of the shop-stewards. We had also written an article for the works magazine in which we outlined the main aims of the project, and pointed out that we would be interviewing between two and three hundred workers randomly selected from the total labour force. Before we approached a respondent we contacted his department's senior supervisor to ensure that the particular job could be covered. The respondent was then brought off the job by the chargehand, and met by the interviewer who discussed the project with him (her) on the way to the interview room. Most of the respondents had no idea that the project was taking place and less idea of why the man in the white coat was taking them toward an office. A number of girls thought that they were in for a medical examination while others felt that they were about to be disciplined or asked to participate in a 'product testing' experiment. These situations, while often humorous at the time, revealed dramatically the intense social isolation associated with work on the production belts. They provided further proof of the 'us and themness' that we had initially observed as characterising the situation of the workers in the large departments.

The Sample

We selected our sample from a sampling frame of all production employees taken from the clock number lists kept by the Personnel Department. This list provided us with information on the department and type of job of each of the workers. We had decided that the orientations toward work of women and men would probably differ, and that the part-time (married) women could be expected to possess work orientations that differed from the full-time (mainly single) women. In addition we suspected that the nature of the work on the night shift would attract workers whose orientations were different from those of the men employed on the day shift. In this assumption we were supported by the different 'character' of the night shift — higher level of unionisation, less adherence to formalised rules, etc. — and by the fact that the mean age of men employed on nights appeared to be significantly higher than that of men on the day shift. We were arguing, therefore, that the work force at Brompton was composed of four distinct groups; men and women with the economic responsibilities of dependent children, and men and women without these, or with less severe, responsibilities. Further, we expected that these groups would possess different orientations toward work, and that there would be an affinity between them and the categories of full- and part-time employment for women and day and night work for men. We will give much greater consideration to the nature and significance of these assumptions in the next chapter; at this time we should point out that they eased considerably the problem of sampling. The sample frame was structured on the basis of these four main categories, and we were easily able to adopt them as the main strata of our sample.

In addition, however, we were aware that the technological structure of the work situation would exert an important influence upon perceptions of work. Therefore we further stratified our sample on the basis of job type. A further complication existed on the day shift where the labour force of each department varied considerably in size. This problem was less significant on the night shift where the total labour force was less than that of one of thé big departments on the day shift. The population on the day shift, therefore, was stratified by department, and a variable sampling fraction was used in the selection of the sample of women.

In addition, we distinguished shop-stewards from other workers and included all this stratum in the sample. However, the information gained from interviews with stewards has only been used to help our general understanding of the situation; it has not been used in the statistical analysis of this report.

Thus, in effect, we drew two separate samples; one comprising of all shop-stewards, and a main sample of all other workers. The latter, we have seen, was stratified by the four main groups, by department and by job type. A sampling fraction of one tenth was used for all strata except those of women in the larger departments, where the fraction was one twentieth. The basic details of the main sample are shown in table 1.1.

Table 1.1 *Main sample*

Group	Population	Selected sample	Contacted sample	% loss	Adjusted sample[15]
Men, days	690	69	64	7%	64
Men, nights	520	52	46	11%	46
Women, full-time	1300	78	67	14%	109
Women, part-time	1070	75	54	28%	78
Total	3580	274	231	16%	297

15 As a variable sampling fraction was used in the selection of the women in the sample, the figures have had to be adjusted in order to ensure consistency between the various groups.

It can be seen from table 1.1 that a sample of 231 workers were interviewed. This represents 6·1% of the total population of production employees. Forty-three of the workers in the original sample of 274 were not contacted. Only in one instance was this due to a worker refusing to be interviewed; in all the other cases failure to contact a respondent was due to the absence of the respondent from the plant due either to a protracted illness or the termination of employment.

It is of interest to note that although the overall sample loss was 16% its distribution between and within our four groups was extremely uneven. The loss on the night shift was larger than that of the men on the day shift. Similarly the loss of part-time women was double that for the full-time women, and within the former group loss on the evening shift was as high as 40%. These variations in the distribution of sample loss are obviously of interest in themselves, as they relate to areas of high labour-turnover and absenteeism. These have been used in other studies[16] as indices of industrial conflict and low worker involvement. Accordingly they should be borne in mind in relation to the evidence we shall present in the following chapters.[17] Their interpretation can be reviewed in the light of this evidence, and vice versa. At the same time they give need for caution since some of those not contacted are likely to have had lower attachment to the firm, introducing some possible bias into our findings.

As this was basically a descriptive and exploratory study we have not considered it appropriate to use any complicated statistical or measurement techniques. In addition to the limitations of our sample, indicated above, we were not in a position to define in advance the precise form of data we should require for such techniques. This being so we saw little point in encumbering the text with the details of statistical analysis. However, in developing the argument, tests of association have been used at appropriate points, and throughout, where the discussion entails relationships between variables (unless the text makes clear an exception), these relationships are significant at the 5% level.[18]

---

16 See, for example, W. H. Scott *et al.*, *Coal and Conflict*; G. K. Ingham, *Size of Industrial Organisation and Worker Behaviour.*
17 However, the association between rate of contact and type of group is never strong. Differences are significant only between men and women and, among the women, between full-time and part-time employees. Thus the only group one can distinguish with confidence in this respect is that of part-time women.
18 Tests of significance were usually chi^2 tests. It should be borne in mind that the variable sampling fractions had to be allowed for in these tests.

Since our interest is in relating variations within the workforce rather than in presenting a picture of Brompton workers, we shall not be directly concerned with the extent to which our sample allows us to give a representative description of the total workforce. At the same time our analysis is set in the context of the complete factory. Therefore, bearing in mind also that we wish to randomise 'errors' due to factors we are not considering, it is important that our sample was drawn randomly and the figures adjusted for the different sampling fractions. This adjusted sample should give a fair representation of the whole, but to a large degree it will be convenient to treat it as though it were a statistical population in itself.

2 The workers at Brompton

The study took place in a factory situated on the fringes of a large industrial conurbation. Employment in the area had been linked historically with a few basic industries. There had been considerable hardship in the 1930s, and since the war it had again taken on many of the features of a depressed area. Rates of unemployment were persistently higher than the national average while the level of wage rates was lower. Housing conditions were bad for large sections of the community and since the war large numbers of working class people had been rehoused in corporation estates around the edge of the city. The factory was located within two miles of such an estate at Brompton, and at the time of the study had a labour force of some three and a half thousand production workers, two thirds of whom were women.

The plant was a subsidiary of William Gourmet & Sons, a large international producer of a range of luxury foods. The company originated as a family firm in the early part of this century. The family's ideology fell within the tradition of enlightened paternalism which is perhaps best typified in England by the Cadbury and Rowntree families.[1] This ideology rejected the moral basis of *laissez faire* capitalism with its belief that authority stemmed axiomatically from ownership, and stressed that employers and employees had basic responsibilities to each other that extended beyond contractual obligations. At their factory in Longborough the Gourmet family provided benefit schemes and leisure activities for their workers, and developed a tradition of consultation which was seen as an important means of obtaining a sense of involvement within the labour force. Like the human relations tradition which it preceded, therefore, the ideology had both practical and moral connotations. The policies seem to have been effective. Many workers, and often whole families spent their lives working for the company, and the history of Longborough was remarkably free of overt industrial conflict.

Since 1945 the company has experienced a period of dramatic change. It has been pushed by the logic of its market position toward vast increases in

---

1 For a discussion of this tradition see, J. Child, *British Management Thought.* Also P. A. Baran and P. M. Sweezy in *Monopoly Capital* Ch. II give a detailed consideration of the position of the family firm in the monopolistic markets of Western Europe and the U.S.A.

its level of output and a high degree of product differentiation, both of which have been achieved through a series of mergers and an expansion of their own plant. These changes were accompanied by an increased emphasis upon professional management and sales techniques which were in turn assisted by the post war developments in management theory. In the face of these changes and the emergence of the welfare state, the tradition of paternalism at Gourmets had proven increasingly difficult to sustain. At the time of the research the rationalisation was incomplete, and the management of the plant at Brompton were experiencing the consequences of the conflicting forces.

When the plant at Brompton was opened, an attempt was made to replicate within it parts of the Longborough tradition. Although the senior management of the plant felt that the welfare state had undermined the significance of the company's benefit schemes they still believed that many of the practices established at Longborough had a place within the modern corporation. The Longborough benefit schemes, works rules, system of payment and consultative machinery were established in the Brompton factory. It appears that the transposition was not entirely successful. While the plant did not experience any period of sustained open conflict, there had been some disagreements over the status of unionism within the factory. Rates of labour turnover were higher than the management had anticipated, and there was a widespread feeling amongst them that relations in the Brompton factory were greatly inferior to those that prevailed in the parent plant. To a large extent this was to be expected. The Gourmet tradition can have had little meaning to Brompton workers at a time when the managerial policies of the firm were in many ways indistinguishable from those of most other large employers. Increasingly, one suspects, the Gourmet tradition was experienced by these workers as peculiar managerial foibles rather than a coherent view of the world.

Given this, however, it is interesting to note that the senior management of the plant explained the problems experienced at Brompton almost entirely by a form of regional ethnocentricity. The workers whom they employed there, they argued, were fundamentally different from those at Longborough; they were especially different in their union-mindedness and their predilection for alcohol. Management used this, in great part, to explain the demands for comparable wage rates with Longborough and the growing pressures from shop-stewards for greater facilities to be made available for recruitment to the union. Now, while it is undoubtedly true that there is a significant regional differentiation of the British working class, this of itself cannot be seen as an adequate explanation of the problems experienced by the management of the Brompton factory. Such problems must also be seen in relation to the work situation, and in addition to considering the social characteristics of the labour force it is necessary to examine the nature of work in the factory, the level of wage payment and the forms of management and trade union organisation.

TECHNOLOGY, WORK AND WAGES

In examining the relationships between people within an institution, it is always advisable to look first at the formally defined responsibilities and rewards that operate within that institution. In examining a factory from this standpoint the workers, in a number of important respects, can be said to experience the same objective situation – the relationship of labour to capital. This relationship can be seen to enter the day to day life of a factory in the form of power relationships and through the rules established within these.

At Brompton many rules applied equally to all workers and served to differentiate them from members of management. Each worker was expected to work a forty-hour week, apart from the part-time women who worked a week of twenty hours composed of five morning, afternoon or evening shifts. At the beginning of each shift the workers walked through the main security gates, through the company playing fields, towards their departments where they clocked their cards and changed into white overalls and caps. The hour was decimalised into units of six minutes, which were used as the basis of deductions incurred through lateness or absence from the job. Every worker who left his department for whatever reason was required to clock his card before doing so.

There are, however, important differences between the situations of workers even at this formal level. At the Brompton factory this was most clearly exemplified on the day shift by the split between men and women who did different types of work, with a lower pay scale for the women. In addition to this, further crucial divisions within the workforce were provided by the existence of a permanent night shift of men, and the employment of many women on part-time shifts during the day. There are numerous sources of differentiation within a factory and it can be expected that the division of labour will contribute to these. At Brompton the relationship between the social characteristics of the workforce and the division of labour was particularly interesting and formed a focus for the study.

The factory was a multi-product one which produced several lines of its main commodities. A useful distinction can be made between the processes which produced these commodities, and those which packed and wrapped them. The former processes were capital intensive and operated by men, the latter labour intensive and operated mainly by women. Production workers on both processes were paid on an incentive bonus scheme.

15

Each of the commodities was manufactured under conditions of continuous flow production. Within the flow the ingredients were mixed and heated and then moulded and decorated. The main jobs involved the selection and measurement of the ingredients and the mechanical regulation of elements in the flow. They were performed by male operatives, occasionally with the help of an assistant. The task involved a degree of training in the job situation and many of the operatives had had experience of similar work in their previous employment. Only a minority of the labour force were involved in these manufacturing processes.

Most of the workers were employed directly on, or supplied materials to, mass production wrapping and packaging systems. It was these systems which dominated the plant. Prepackaging has been associated with the increase in product differentiation within the industry and has in turn affected the nature of work and the social composition of the workforce. The commodities were packed by hand by groups of workers who sat alongside conveyor belts. The tasks were essentially repetitive, each worker packing one item and each task relying for its performance upon the successful completion of the preceding one. The wrapping operations were more mechanised but no less repetitive. Groups of four or five workers performed various tasks around a machine which wrapped the product in paper or cellophane. In addition to these two main operations, other workers were employed to 'service' the machines and packing belts with the manufactured products, and others to weigh and check the finished commodities. All these jobs were constrained by the demands of the mass production technology, mostly to a high degree, with little skill involved and the pace of work decisively influenced by the speed of the belts and machines.[2]

On the day shift the packing and wrapping operations were performed by women who were employed as either full-time or part-time workers. Young unmarried women dominated the former group while the latter was composed almost entirely of married women with children. The firm had been forced to rely increasingly upon the employment of married women and had developed a system of three part-time shifts — mornings, afternoons and evenings — as an aid to recruitment. These women tended to work separately from the full-time women so that, as a rule, a work group would be composed entirely of full-time or part-time workers. The dominance of women in the main production departments was interrupted only by the men and youths — known as 'juniors' — who assisted in the servicing of the machines and belts. On the night shift, however, because of legal restrictions and a national agreement, *all* workers were male and over the age of twenty-one, most of them performing tasks done by women and youths on the day shift.

2 See e.g. D. Bell, 'Work and its Discontents', in *The End of Ideology.*

Jobs

These points can be made clearer by examining the distribution of work tasks amongst the workers in the sample. We may distinguish three main types of job — operator, belt-work and time work. However, when we look more closely at these types we find appreciable variation within them in the actual content of jobs. Accordingly each has been split into two distinct categories giving the following pairs — process and machine operators, direct belt workers and auxiliaries, and manual and non-manual time workers. We have included both wrappers and packers in the category of direct belt workers since their jobs are essentially the same. These occupational categories were unevenly distributed between the four main groups of our sample and in some cases there were further differences in the nature of the work. The details of this division of labour are contained in table 2.1. It will be seen that another category has been used for workers who had yet to be allocated a permanent job, but as they were all employed as belt workers — although not on any one particular belt — their number can for most purposes be added to the second occupational type; on the day shift normally as auxiliaries and at nights as direct belt workers.

Table 2.1   *Divisions of labour*

	Day men	Night men	Full-time women	Part-time women	All
1a Operator: process	13	2	—	—	15
1b Operator: machine	—	6	16	6	28
2a Belt worker: direct	8	18	51	47	124
2b Belt worker: auxiliary	20	3	20	13	56
3a Time worker: manual	12	7	6	—	25
3b Time worker: non-manual	10	5	11	2	28
4 No permanent job	1	5	5	10	21
Total	64	46	109	78	297

Among those classed as operators we see a marked difference between the day men and the rest. The men on the day shift were employed as operators on the process technology, while those in the other three groups, apart from two night-shift men, were operators of wrapping machines. On a wrapping machine an operator was the leading hand of a team of four or five who

17

worked continually throughout the shift wrapping the products. In contrast the process operator was in no way tied to a machine; he worked alone or with an assistant and had a much greater freedom of movement.

The next pair of categories — direct and auxiliary belt workers — is probably the most homogeneous of the three. All workers in these categories were involved in the packing and wrapping operations. It is important, however, to make a distinction between the two categories, i.e. between those workers whose jobs tied them directly to the belt, and those who merely 'serviced' these operations. The former groups of workers were in the machine-paced, single location situation which is generally thought of as typical of the intrinsically unrewarding 'belt' or 'track' work. The service workers, on the other hand, had a certain freedom to move around and were not directly paced by the machine. Thus they were in a situation which has generally been regarded as leading to relatively greater satisfaction,[3] though we shall see the position was not so straightforward here. In both groups of women, auxiliaries were outnumbered by belt-tied workers about 2 : 1, they always worked close to the belts and they were integrated into the groups of direct belt workers for whom they serviced. Among the men it was rather different. The nature of the servicing operations were such that a comparatively small night shift could be 'carried' to some extent by the servicing done on the day shift. So, while most of the men concerned with belt work on the day shift were auxiliaries, eighteen of the twenty-one on the night shift were either packers or wrappers, and to this number can be added the five workers who had no permanent job but were continually employed in jobs directly on the belts. The male belt auxiliaries usually moved over much greater areas than the women, and so were much more independent of both the belts themselves and the people who worked on them.

An important division also exists within our third pair of categories of work — 'time work'. The distinctive feature of all these jobs is that they were not directly related to the production process, so that the incentive payment system which operated for production workers would have been inappropriate. Two very different types of workers were in this position, however, and the numbers were split fairly evenly between them. The first type were hourly paid manual workers; these were almost exclusively cleaners, most of whom had never worked as production workers in the Brompton factory. The other group, which can, perhaps, be termed 'non-manual' was mainly composed of factory records clerks and inspectors who recorded and made checks upon the weight, quality and flow of the products through their departments. Some of these workers had been employed in production work in the factory

---

3 See, e.g. E. Chinoy, *Automobile Workers and the American Dream.*

and had been promoted to their present jobs. The differences between the cleaners and this latter group are fundamental ones. The cleaners were paid less and had less status and power than the records clerks and inspectors. Accordingly we might expect the attitudes of these two types of workers to vary considerably, and we shall draw attention to the most important of these differences in the pages that follow.

A further point needs to be made with respect to the time workers. It can be seen from table 2.1 that these categories of work were unevenly distributed between our four main groups of workers. Only two of the part-time workers were paid on time-rates; both of these being factory records clerks. While a greater percentage of the full-time women were so employed (16%), this is much lower than the figures recorded by both groups of men – day men 34% and night men 26%. These differences are due in part to the fact that many of the cleaning operations involved a degree of heavy, greasy work which was thought to be more appropriate for men than women. When comparison is restricted to the distribution of non-manual time workers the differences all but disappear, although the men are still marginally better represented.

Pay

A basic aspect of the work situation is the payment system. At Brompton all the workers received their pay in envelopes from their charge-hand, during the Friday shift, as they worked at their jobs. The money in these envelopes was calculated by means of extremely complicated systems of individual and group incentive bonus schemes. Our study, in fact, revealed that while the shop-stewards understood the payment system, almost none of the rank and file workers did. This was a perpetual source of antagonism in the factory which is discussed in chapter 4.

A new national agreement had been negotiated a few months prior to the study, and the base rates are contained in table 2.2. These rates applied to men and women over the age of 21 who had served a probationary period in

Table 2.2 *Payment of production workers, base rates per forty hours*

Grade of work	Men	Women
1	£15·75	–
2	£15·25	£10·12½
3	£14·75	£9·75
4	£14·25	£9·37½

the factory. Workers under the age of 21 were paid on 'junior rates' which moved upwards in annual increments from the 16-year-old rate. Part-time employees earned approximately half the rates quoted for women in the table and the men on the night shift earned a 'night allowance' of 280 pence above the rates paid to men on days.

There were four grades of production work, with the scale of payment for women approximately two-thirds of the male rate. The grades were related to the categories of work employed in table 2.1. Most belt workers were classed as Grade 3 while a minority of the auxiliaries were classed as Grade 4. Only operators on the process technology were Grade 1 — note the absence of a Grade 1 for women — while the other operators were paid at Grade 2. The payment of cleaners approximated to the Grade 4 rate and inspectors the Grade 2 rate.

The figures given in table 2.2 are base rates for forty hours, i.e. they are notional amounts of what the incentive payments should yield for a normal week's work. In practice men could usually earn about £1.50, and women about £1.25, above these rates, plus any premium payment for nightwork or overtime. At this time the average earnings for all manual workers per forty hours were £17·45 for men and £10·37 for full-time women.[4] Thus it appears that most of the women but only the top earning men were receiving more than the average. However, these figures are not strictly comparable since the national figures are based on hourly averages which include overtime and other premium payments, thereby giving a higher figure. Furthermore, they are for all manual wage earners, including skilled workers, whereas the Gourmet rates are for semi-skilled and unskilled only. This makes little difference for the women's earnings, although it is likely that the rates at Gourmets would not appear so favourable if the comparison were limited to factory work. For the men, however, the point is quite important. It means that the day-men's wages were probably not very different from the national average for the sort of jobs they could get, while the night-shift workers were clearly better paid.

We should also take account of regional variation in earnings, since to a large extent workers use a local, rather than national frame of reference in evaluating a job. In fact Brompton is in a relatively low wage area, where the rates for men per forty hours were about 60p below the national average. Thus the Brompton rates compared rather more favourably with the regional rates. On the other hand the Gourmet management responded to regional variations, and the wages at Brompton were about 8% below those paid at

---

4 *Ministry of Labour Gazette*, Jan. 1967, p. 79. The figure for women covers workers aged 18 and over.

the parent plant in Longborough. Not surprisingly, this was a source of conflict, with pressure from the union to remove this differential.

Altogether the wages at Brompton were not particularly high, but they were rather better than usual in the region and compared favourably with those offered elsewhere in the Brompton area. For the women there was little other factory work available, and the Gourmet rates were distinctly better than they were likely to get in the main alternatives, such as shop work or office cleaning. The wage rates of the men on the day shift were generally a little better than those for comparable jobs elsewhere, while the night men would have difficulty in finding the same wages in another job in the area.

Some general observations can now be made upon the division of labour in the Brompton factory. We have seen that technology was potentially an important source of differentiation, at least in so far as it distinguished the main types of production work. Also differences in sex and age would seem to be important elements of the social context, because of their relation to position in the production process. The opportunity to work nights and the allocation of job tasks on days were largely determined by these criteria. Furthermore, wages varied not only with jobs but also with sex and age.

Two pay structures operated within the factory, one for the females and a higher one for the males. Both part-time and full-time women were paid the same rates although the part-time women enjoyed fewer and less adequate fringe benefits. Also both groups of women tended to be employed in similar work. On the day shift there were clearly located areas of 'women's work', the mass production units being dominated by women − over 90% of the women were employed on, or in jobs auxiliary to, the packing and wrapping units. There were differences in the formal positions of the full-time and part-time women, however. The part-time women were more likely not to be employed in a permanent job − 13% compared with only 5% of the full-time women[5] − and more likely to be employed on the belt rather than as operators or time workers.

A further point of some importance is that part-time and full-time women tended to be separated from each other in the work situation. Most work groups of women were entirely composed of one or the other type of worker, and in the larger departments this pattern of segregation was extended − whole sections of these departments were dominated either by the full-time or the part-time women.

The full significance of sex differences in the work situation may be seen in the clear distinction which existed between 'men's work' and 'women's

---

5 The difference was not statistically significant in our sample but was general throughout the factory.

work' on the day shift. The men who came into most contact with the women were the belt auxiliaries, but although both sexes were employed as auxiliaries to women packers and wrappers, the division was maintained. Many of the servicing operations involved quite heavy work and all these tasks were performed by male workers. One such task involved the 'trucking' of large wooden trolleys loaded with packed or wrapped produce from the ends of the belts to departmental storage bays. The difference between the auxiliary operations performed by males and females was heightened by the fact that the women could be asked, and in fact expected to be asked, to work on the belts at some time, whereas there was every expectation that the men would not be so asked.

While the packing and wrapping operations on the day shift were clearly defined as 'women's work', the men had exclusive right to the jobs on the process technology. Many of these were the highest paid jobs open to production workers on the day shift. All Grade 1 work was located within the process sections and was performed by men. The men who worked as auxiliaries on the belts, therefore, might aspire to these jobs rather than the ones on the belt, though their chances were reduced by the firm's tendency to recruit experienced operators from outside. They did have a further alternative, however. If they were over 21, they could have opted for a job on the night shift.

The strict differentiation of task that operated on the day shift was obviously impossible on nights. The men on nights were paid an additional allowance, they had Saturday, Sunday and most of Monday free of work and in return they performed the tasks that were performed by women on the day shift. Half the men on the night shift worked as packers and wrappers on the belts while a further 13% performed 'operator' tasks that were restricted to women on the day shift. Altogether about three-quarters of the men on nights were employed on 'women's work'. Here it can be noted that the notion of 'women's work' involved the shop-stewards of the night shift in a contradictory position in their bargaining with management. The men on the shift felt that the night allowance was in part a payment for performing 'women's work'; management for its part regularly countered with the suggestion that they should be paid less as the girls on days performed the same tasks more efficiently.

At this formal level, then, it seems clear that strong lines of differentiation existed within the Brompton labour force. Also it can be seen that the four employment categories — men on day and night work; women on part-time and full-time work — provided the basis for significant subgroupings of workers. This is not to say that other groupings were irrelevant. The departments differed in size and to some extent in production process. The organisation of work also created occupational divisions which tended to cut across our four groups, although the work of the full-time and part-time women and the night shift men was essentially the same, being dominated by the wrapping and packing units. Although these divisions were of some importance, managerial policies on job-manning together with government regulation of the hours worked by women and distinctions made between 'men's work' and 'women's work', had combined in a way which suggests that the main source of affective ties for the worker at Brompton would be within one of our four groups rather than within, say, occupational groups. Similarly it seems likely that these same influences would have contributed to these groups being distinguished by particular types of workers' interests and expectations. Elements within the situation invite a comparison with van den Berghe's discussion of certain multi-racial situations. His notion of structural pluralism, where the 'social structure is compartmentalised into analogous, parallel, non-complementary but distinguishable sets of institutions',[6] has some relevance here. Although there are fundamental differences between this type of situation and that at Brompton, it is interesting to note that as well as being paid on different rates, men and women were hired, fired and had their problems dealt with by different branches of the Personnel Department. Also the worker's job career was likely to develop within one of the four employment categories, each of which tended to have its own line of supervision below departmental manager.

We might expect, therefore, that the workforce at Brompton would be typified by a degree of cultural heterogeneity, and that the subcultures would be related to the four employment categories that we have mentioned. This claim becomes more plausible when we turn to examine the social characteristics of the workers in the sample.

SOCIAL CHARACTERISTICS OF THE WORKFORCE

We have argued that the social characteristics of workers are important for two reasons; as aspects their biographies influencing orientations to work, and as components of the social context at work. Accordingly, we are interested in both the nature of these characteristics and their distribution within the workforce.

To some extent they help to produce a common understanding of work. The experience of a shared class position, which arises from power relations in the organisation of work, is reinforced by many aspects of working-class life outside of work. Such common class experience is further emphasised

6 See P. L. Van den Berghe, *Race and Racism*, p. 34.

where workers come together in the life of a community. Now, while it would be difficult to argue that all the workers at Brompton belonged to the same community, it is of some importance that over 70% of the sample lived in an area with a three mile radius which included the factory. Furthermore, large numbers of the workers had friends or kin working in the factory. The proximity of the factory to home and the presence of friends there were, in fact, the two most common reasons given for choosing Gourmets as a place of work.

On the other hand there are many personal forces deriving from, say, the individual's understanding of himself or herself as a father, sister, lover or friend, which may be expected to lead to diverse perceptions of work. It will, therefore, be useful to outline such features as the age and family situation of the workers, and to relate them to the division of labour. Undoubtedly sex is one fundamental social characteristic, which we have seen is also basic to the division of labour. We shall keep in mind the division by sex in the following discussion, but will also further divide the men into day and night shifts and the women into full-time and part-time shifts to give our four main employment categories.

Perhaps the most generally relevant social characteristic is age, since it is related to so many aspects of a person's experience. In the first place it indicates his generation and the period he has lived through. Thus we can hardly expect those who have lived through two world wars and the depression to view their employment in the same light as young workers born after 1945. Similarly, age is closely related to the length of time a man has spent in work, though the connection is much weaker for women. Many studies have shown that expectations from work vary with age, as older workers tend to be more easily satisfied. However it is not clear whether this is directly age or length of work life; is it a 'mellowing' of outlook, are their aspirations beaten down by the need to adjust to the limited rewards attainable, or have they finally found a satisfactory job?

The way a worker feels about his job is undoubtedly influenced by his socialisation in the job. Thus length of service in a particular job − or, at a different level, in a particular firm − is liable to have a bearing on his attitudes. This, again, is dependent on age, particularly among younger workers.

Probably the most important social characteristic − once again related to age − is position in the life cycle. In relation to work-life we may distinguish five stages. First there is the period before marriage, when financial responsibilities are low; then there are the years of marriage before starting a family; then the period when the children are young and the wife is at home to care for them; as the children grow older, and make still greater demands on the family finances, the mother may return to work; finally the children grow up and become independent, after which the mother is free to work if she wishes, the financial pressures are eased and the next landmark ahead is retirement. Of course, not everyone passes through this cycle; many remain single, marriages may remain childless, while some people have dependants other than children. However, it is clear that the family position, whatever it may be, is liable to have a deep influence on each individual's view of the world in general and work in particular.

We will start, therefore, by looking at the age distribution of the sample. Then we shall consider family position and finally length of service at Gourmets. We shall look to see how these variables relate to the different types of jobs, and how they combine in our four groups.

Age

The age distributions are given in table 2.3. Comparing the distributions of men and women we see there was not a lot of difference, except for a much larger proportion of men over the age of 50, 24% of the men compared with only 7% of the women. This was due entirely to the large number of cleaners in the older age group since, as we saw earlier, these jobs were nearly all done by men. Apart from this, the main differences emerge from comparison between the two groups of men and between the two groups of women.

Table 2.3 *Age distribution of the sample*

	Men			Women		
Age	Day	Night	All	Full-time	Part-time	All
Under 20 years	17	–	17	34	–	34
20-29 years	17	3	20	23	4	27
30-39 years	6	11	17	22	18	40
40-49 years	9	21	30	24	49	73
50 years and over	15	11	26	6	7	13
Total	64	46	110	109	78	187

The differences between the two groups of men are quite pronounced; much more so than would follow simply from the age restriction on night work. All but 7% of the night shift were over the age of 30, while 53% of the men on days were under this age. Again the over 50 age group is an exception because of the number of elderly cleaners. We now see that it is among the men of the day shift that they make the age group disproportionately large. If we exclude the cleaners, the age differences between shifts become much more marked, with the night worker typically in his forties and the day man between 15 and 30.

A similar comparison can be made between the two groups of women. More than half of the full-time women were under 30 while only 5% of the part-time women were under that age. It will be useful to relate the ages of the workers to their jobs.

Table 2.4   *The age and occupation of full-time women*

Type	Age					Total
	Under 20	20-29	30-39	40-49	Over 50	
1. Operator	–	3	2	9	2	16
2. Belt worker	32	17	13	9	–	71
3. Time worker	1	3	5	4	4	17
4. No perm. job	1	–	2	2	–	5
Total	34	23	22	24	6	109

Table 2.5   *Age and occupation of part-time women*

Type	Age					Total
	Under 20	20-29	30-39	40-49	Over 50	
1. Operator	–	–	3	3	–	6
2. Belt worker	–	3	14	36	7	60
3. Time worker	–	–	–	2	–	2
4. No perm. job	–	1	1	8	–	10
Total	–	4	18	49	7	78

It can be seen from table 2.5 that the typical part-time woman worker at Brompton worked on the belts and was aged between 30 and 50 years. If we include the women with no permanent job we find that 76% of all part-time women workers come into this category. However, it is much more difficult to make generalisations about the women who were employed full-time. We have already noted that over half (52%) of this group were under 30, and to this may be added the fact that 86% of these young women worked on the belts. We would expect, therefore, that these workers would form the most significant grouping among the full-time women. Their dominance within the group however, was, numerically at least, much less decisive than that of the middle aged belt workers within the group of part-time women. Belt workers were clearly the main occupational group of full-time women, but a third of them were over 30.

Furthermore, when we consider the full-time operators and time workers we find that more than three-quarters of them were over 30, and most were over 40. This is hardly surprising since they were employed on the better paid, more responsible jobs. However, it does indicate an occupational minority who were significantly older than the other full-time women, yet doing jobs which were rarely held by part-time women.

While it is reasonable to point out the differences in the mean ages of each of the groups of women, and to point to the dominance of young belt workers amongst the full-time women and middle-aged belt workers amongst the part-time women, we will need to bear in mind that a substantial proportion of the women who were employed full-time did not fit the dominant pattern. We can pursue these points further when we consider the family circumstances of the workers.

Table 2.6 *Family background of the sample*

Family structure	Day men	Night men	Full-time women	Part-time women	All
Single	28	6	58	–	92
Married:					
No dependent children	18	17	30	26	91
1 dependent child	7	10	8	16	41
2 dependent children	9	7	10	17	43
Over 2 dependent children	2	6	3	19	30
Total	64	46	109	78	297

Family

As we would expect, the pattern of family dependence was related to the age distribution of the workforce. We have already noted the high proportion of young men and adolescents on the day shift, so we would expect there to be many more single men on this shift than on the night shift, and this was, in fact, the case. All of the day men under 20 were single, as were half those between 20 and 30, but very few of the older men; in fact 93% of the single men on the day shift were under 30. Of all the day men 44% were unmarried and only a little over a quarter of them had dependent children. In contrast, the handful of single men on the night shift were spread over the whole age range, while the great majority were married and half of them had dependent children. In both groups most of the older men employed as time-workers had grown-up families, and once again if we exclude these men the pattern becomes clearer. The day men were mostly single or married with young families, while the men on nights were at a later stage in the life-cycle. The night men were more likely to have completed their families, their children were growing up, and some had started work. A few of the men had, quite recently, seen all their children become financially independent of them.

On both shifts the operators tended to be slightly older than the belt workers, and were further advanced in the life-cycle. This was particularly marked on the day shift, where all but one of the thirteen operators were over 20 and married, while ten of them had families, including seven of the eleven men on the shift with two or more children. Thus, although they were younger than the night belt workers, they had reached similar stages of family responsibility. The contrast between shifts, therefore, is to be seen most clearly among the belt workers, with mostly family men on nights and the day men predominantly single.

The two groups of women were also differentiated by family position in combination with age. Thus, over half of the full-time women were unmarried while no woman who worked part-time was single. Of the full-time women who were unmarried, 81% were under the age of 25, while no part-time woman was under this age. This comparison reflects the polarity between the 'typical' full-time and part-time woman worker — the former single and working until the time she marries and has children; the latter returning to work after she has married and had children. It will be useful to look more closely at this relationship between age and family structure, paying particular attention to the full-time women over 30 who would appear, *prima facie*, to have more in common with women of their own generation who worked part-time.

Two main points of comparison arise out of tables 2.7 and 2.8. Firstly, it can be seen that although similar proportions of part-time and full-time

Table 2.7 *Age and family structure: full-time women*

Family structure	Age					Total
	20	20-29	30-39	40-49	Over 50	
Single	34	15	4	3	2	58
Married:						
No dependent children	–	7	9	11	3	30
1 dependent child	–	1	2	4	1	8
2 dependent children	–	–	4	6	–	10
Over 2 dependent children	–	–	3	–	–	3
Total	34	23	22	24	6	109

Table 2.8 *Age and family structure: part-time women*

Family structure	Age					Total
	20	20-29	30-39	40-49	Over 50	
Single	–	–	–	–	–	–
Married						
No dependent children	–	–	2	17	7	26
1 dependent child	–	1	3	12	–	16
2 dependent children	–	1	4	12	–	17
Over 2 dependent children	–	2	9	8	–	19
Total	–	4	18	49	7	78

married women were without dependent children (33% and 28% respectively) these statistics conceal quite fundamental differences. Almost all the part-time women in this position were over 40 years old, each one of them having raised children who had since begun to work. On the other hand, over half of the full-time women without dependent children were under the age of 40, and of these only two had children – each having a 17-year-old boy, while a further three of the fourteen over 40 had no children.

When we allow for age differences we still find considerable differences between the groups in terms of family structures. Even among the under 30s there is a marked difference as all four part-time workers had children, compared with only one out of fifty-seven full-time women, though eight of them were married. Turning to the women over 30 we see that 65% of the part-time women still had dependent children, and about a quarter of them had at least three children who were still dependent. Among the full-time women in this age range the pattern was rather different. A mere 6% had as many as three dependent children, while only 38% had any at all; the majority were childless and 17% were unmarried. We see, therefore, that typically the full-time women were at an earlier stage in the family cycle than the part-time women, with a minority who seemed likely to remain single. Whereas the women of the part-time shifts had returned to paid employment after a spell at home looking after a young family, the majority of those employed full-time had been working since they left school, though many of them were likely to leave for family reasons at some future date.

There are, of course, familiar reasons for these differences, to be found in the work and family roles of women in our society. We have elaborated the differences here to help justify our claim that useful comparisons can be made between the attitudes of the women in each of these groups.

Relating family position to job for the part-time women workers reveals nothing new. This group is the most homogeneous of the four. All had children and in most cases the children were still dependent; in fact the part-time women tended to have more children than any other group. At the same time almost all of them were employed as belt workers on the wrapping and packing machines. There was no apparent difference in the family positions of these belt workers and the few operators and time workers who worked part-time.

We can learn more of the full-time women by such a comparison, however, and the relevant data is contained in table 2.9. The first point to note is the large proportion of single women employed on belt work. In contrast to the other occupations, the great majority of belt workers were unmarried and seven of the twelve married women without dependent children had married comparatively recently. This is, of course, in keeping with the tendency for belt workers to be younger than the rest. The operators were not significantly different from the rest of the group, although the fact that only one had dependent children is consistent with this being a promotion for women committed to full-time employment.

A rather different pattern is revealed by the women time workers. Only two (12%) of these women, as compared with 61% of all other full-time women, were single, while ten of them were married with dependent children.

Table 2.9 *Family structure and occupation of full-time women*

Job type	Single	Married				All
		No dependent children	1 dependent child	2 dependent children	Over 2 dependent children	
1. Operator	6	9	–	1	–	16
2. Belt worker	49	12	4	4	2	71
3. Time worker	2	5	4	5	1	17
4. No perm. job	1	4	–	–	–	5
Total	58	30	8	10	3	109

Married women with dependent children formed a minority of the full-time labour force at Gourmets, and in our sample they were almost evenly distributed between time workers and the rest. It is not entirely clear why the time workers should be atypical of their group, but it may be a consequence of the different content of their work, since it was mainly the non-manual time workers who had dependent families. Their jobs involved a fair degree of clerical competence, so it is probable that these women were recruited from a different section of the labour market with relevant clerical experience or qualifications, and with different needs and expectations. If they wanted clerical jobs their choice was limited. Apart from one or two non-manual jobs on the part-time production shifts, there was no part-time clerical work at Gourmets. Part-time jobs elsewhere were likely to entail a substantial amount of travelling, which would reduce the advantage of shorter hours. It was against this background that these mothers chose to take full-time factory clerical jobs.

Length of service
Further light can be thrown on the nature of the relationships so far discussed if we consider the length of service of the various workers. The data for the four main groups are summarised in table 2.10.
There are broad similarities between the groups in the pattern of length of service. All groups, for example, had a predominance of workers with comparatively short service in the company. Seventy-eight per cent of the part-time women had been working at Gourmets for less than three years, for the day men and full-time women the proportions were over 60% and on the night shift just under half. The smaller proportion of short service workers on the night shift was offset by a larger proportion of long service workers. A

Table 2.10 *Length of service*

Length of service	Day men	Night men	Full-time women	Part-time women	All
Under 1 year	17	8	20	23	68
1-3 years	22	14	49	38	123
3-5 years	9	5	14	11	39
5-7 years	12	4	10	2	28
Over 7 years	4	15	16	4	39
Total	64	46	109	78	297

third of the night men as compared with 26% of the day men, 15% of the full-time women and only 5% of the part-time women had over seven years service at Brompton.

At this point the greater commitment to occupational careers of the full-time women operators emerges strongly. All sixteen were included in the twenty-six full-time women with over five years service. In keeping with this we may recall their tendency to be older and their lack of dependants. But if this differentiates them from the other full-time women, it also differentiates them from the part-time women, in spite of the similarity of ages.

The night-shift operators also had longer service than most of the men on their shift. All had been with the company for over five years, all but one of them for over seven years. There is no comparable pattern among the day men where only four of the thirteen operatives had worked at Brompton for over five years. The difference here is related to the nature of the operator's task on the day shift. Unlike the other operators at Gourmets[7] these men worked on the process technology and their jobs required a degree of judgement that is associated with experience and training. As a result many of these operatives were recruited by the company from other firms in the area that used similar processes. Consequently, the pattern of 'promotion' that accompanied length of service in production jobs on the night shift and amongst the women was complicated for belt workers on the day shift. While the competent belt worker on the night shift could reasonably hope to be promoted, in time, to 'operator' tasks on the mass-production technology, promotion was much less likely for the young man on days, where movement into operator tasks on the process technology was restricted by skill criteria.

7 Apart from the two process operators working at night.

A further point can be made about the long-service men on the night shift. Many of the men with children at work came into this long-service group. Thus, when they joined the company their children were still dependent, and since then they had seen some or even all their children grow up and leave school.[8] If, for example, we look at the family responsibilities of the operatives at the time they joined Gourmets we see they had just as many dependent children as the belt workers on their shift.

So far we have argued that although certain structural aspects of the workers' situation create the basis for a unifying class experience, strong sources of differentiation can be located within that experience. At Brompton such variables as age, sex, family position and length of service were structured into the formal work organisation in such a way as might be expected to produce basic divisions in the understanding of work. In particular it could be expected that each of the four employment categories – day and night men; full- and part-time women – would provide a focus for such differences, although there would be differences within groups as well.

THE TRADE UNION

At this point it becomes important to examine the position of the trade union in the social context of the Brompton factory. Historically trade unions were developed by workers to give substance to the unifying features of their work situation. They are based on common interests deriving from a shared class position, and their strength is dependent on how workers perceive their situation. To a large extent the workers create the unionisation of their workplace, although within the constraints of the national organisation and characters of available unions. In turn the unionisation is part of the social context influencing workers' overall understanding of work. We will, therefore, look briefly at the pattern of unionisation here. Then, in chapter 6 we will return to the subject for a detailed analysis of the workers' relations with their union.

At Brompton all production workers were represented by the Transport and General Workers Union, which had a branch based on the factory. From the start management had recognised the union at Brompton, as they had for many years previously at Longborough. In general, relations between the company and the union were friendly, but for some time there had been a certain tension in the relations at Brompton and the union was prepared to take militant action. In fact there was a strike during the period of our fieldwork (see chapter 6).

---

8 This does not appear to be the case among the full-time women.

Rather less than half the sample were union members, though the union's success in recruiting varied considerably throughout the labour force. As table 2.11 shows, the night shift was the most strongly unionised of our four

Table 2.11   *Union membership*

	Day men	Night men	Full-time women	Part-time women	All
Members	43	34	38	23	138
Ex-members	8	7	18	4	37
Non-members	13	5	53	51	122
Total	64	46	109	78	297

groups with 74% of their number in the union; this compares with 67% of the day men, 35% of the full-time women and 29% of the part-time women. It is interesting to note that in all but the group of part-time women quite a large proportion — about 15% — of the workers were lapsed members of the union.

The belt workers were the least unionised occupational group with a membership completeness of only 37%. This tendency was most striking among the men of the day shift where only half the belt workers were members compared with 80% of the operatives and time workers. To some extent the explanation lies in length of service, for belt workers generally had not been with the firm as long as other workers, and understandably those with short service were less likely to be members. In fact three-quarters of the workers who had been at Gourmets for less than a year were non-members. The contrast is most striking among the women where only 7% of these new entrants had joined compared with 40% of the rest. There was little noticeable difference with length of service on the night shift, but on days less than half the men with less than a year's service were members compared with 84% of those who had been in the firm for three years or more. This tendency for involvement in the union to increase with service in the company was borne out by the fact that the majority of shop-stewards in the factory had worked there for over five years.

In view of the variation in the strength of unionism, it appears that the union organisation at Brompton was unable to transcend the differences which existed between sections of the workforce. Unionisation seems to have been a further source of differentiation, rather than of unity.

SUMMARY

It will be useful at this point to bring together the main characteristics of the social context of the Brompton factory.

On the basis of the worker's formal relationship with the company we maintained that the workforce could be divided into four main groups – men on the day and night shift; women in full- and part-time employment. Although there was little basis for a conflict of interest to exist between each of these groups it seemed that the system of job allocation, the differential rates of payment and the pattern of interaction at work would combine to make these groups the main points of reference for workers within the factory. This being so we would expect different perceptions of work to be current in each group, and also for the groups to attract employees with different expectations from work. This would lead to four relatively distinct subcultures with 'core' members in each group who dominated the particular subculture.

Following this reasoning we have looked at the composition of our groups, considering the variations in work and especially the variations in the social characteristics of the workers, since the hypothesis that such social characteristics greatly influence expectations is central to our analysis. The data we have presented do indicate some quite fundamental differences between the core members of each group. On the other hand, not surprisingly, we saw the groups were not completely homogeneous nor entirely distinct.

At a very general level the different roles of the sexes in the wider society distinguish between the groups of men and women. Cutting across this distinction, and so separating the four groups is the fact that workers on the night shifts and the part-time women tended to be at a later stage in the life-cycle than the other two groups. The day men were further differentiated by their work, for while the relations of the other groups to the production process were essentially similar, the day men had their own types of work which gave them greater freedom and autonomy. Finally the part-time women were, of course, distinguished from the rest by spending appreciably less time at work.

In addition to these basic differences we saw the groups differed in other ways. But also there were areas where identification might transcend the boundaries of the groups, as for example, the adolescent workers of both sexes on the day shift. In addition there were lines of possible differentiation and conflict within the groups. It will be useful therefore, to review the salient features of each of the groups.

Part-time women. These women formed the most homogeneous of our four groups. They were all married and had raised or were in the process of raising

35

children. Also, because of the difficulty of going out to work even part-time when children are very young, we found few of them were under the age of 30. All of them worked in the mass-production areas, mostly as belt workers. They were more likely to be without a permanent job than any other category of worker and less likely to be an operative or time worker. Few of them had worked for any length of time in the Brompton factory and most of them were not members of a union.

Full-time women. A strong contrast exists between the 'core' members of this group and the 'core' of the previous group. These were young women and adolescent girls working on the packing and wrapping belts. They differed from the part-time women in that they had yet to marry or, if they were married, to have children. However, by no means all the full-time women were typical in this way. For example, some of the belt workers were older and a few had dependent children. There were two important minorities which differed appreciably from the core of the group. Firstly, there were a number of somewhat older women without dependent children and unlikely to have any in the future. Either they had returned to work after their children had grown up or they were unlikely to start a family, usually because they were single women who had passed the 'normal' marrying age. For such women work is likely to be more central in their lives. We saw that many of them had already been working in the factory for some time and were employed on the better paid, more responsible operative jobs. The second small subgroup was due to the presence of the non-manual time workers, most of whom had family responsibilities more like the part-time women than their full-time workmates. Thus this subgroup comprised married women time workers with children who, for the most part, were still at school. We have suggested that, because of the nature of the work, these women were recruited from a section of the labour market with different previous experience – often, in fact, in clerical work where they had acquired different orientations to work. Although it is possible they might have preferred a part-time shift if there had been clerical jobs available, they had, in fact, chosen full-time employment. In view of their choice to work full-time while their children were still young, it seems likely that work was either a central interest or a greater economic necessity in their lives. These three subgroups, the large core of young women and the two minorities of older women, as we have specified them, accounted for the great majority of the full-time women.

Night men. This group of men is interesting for two main reasons. Firstly it was almost completely isolated from the other groups of workers and also from the higher management of the factory. We might expect, therefore, that such isolation would lead to increased group solidarity and also a loosening of managerial control over the shift. The second point relates to the fact that these men were employed in the same jobs, on the same machinery, as the women who worked during the day. Although the technological implications approach would lead us to expect similarities in the responses of these groups to the work situation, it would seem that the isolation of the night shift, together with the definition of packing and wrapping jobs as 'women's work', would lead to quite important differences between the night men and the women. Further to this, we noted that the men on the night shift tended to be older and have larger dependent families than their male colleagues on the day shift. These dependants would, we expect, have been an important factor contributing to the choice of their present employment. A further indication of the nature of these differences is to be found in the fact that the night shift had a higher percentage of union members than any of the other groups, and that a large number of the night workers had been working in the factory for well over five years.

We can sum up the 'core' member of the night shift as a middle aged family man engaged on 'women's work' and a union member. Although less homogeneous than the part-time women, the combination of relative isolation with the other factors did produce a definite group with, as we shall see, its own subculture.

Day men. While men on the day shift were younger and less likely to be married than the men on the night shift, we were able to isolate two 'core' groups among these men – the young men and youths who acted as auxiliaries to the mass production operations, and the operators on the process technology. The larger group of belt workers tended to be younger and were mostly single, while the process operators were typically married with dependent children. The operators' jobs were of higher status and better paid, but promotion chances for the belt auxiliaries were limited by a tendency to recruit operatives directly from outside. These differences might possibly lead to separate identifications and conflict of interests within the group of men on the day shift. Perhaps an indication of this is to be found in the comparatively low level of unionisation achieved amongst the 'belt workers', who in addition to having a high percentage of non-members also contained most of the defaulted membership amongst the day men. Further to this we can note that half of the shop-stewards amongst this group were employed as operatives.

However, we should not overlook the distinctive shared characteristics which made the core subgroups similar. They were all employed on 'men's work' which was identified as something quite distinct from the work of the women. This work, in both occupational subgroups, gave the men much greater autonomy and freedom of movement than enjoyed by workers in any of the other groups. Also, in spite of different family positions, there was considerable overlap in the age ranges of belt workers and operatives.

A final point to make here is that both groups of men had a large contingent of manual time workers. These men were usually employed as cleaners, they were mostly over the age of 50 and had worked in the factory for over five years. While not particularly different from the other men of the night shift, they were distinctly different from both 'core' types of the day shift.

This chapter has indicated that the four groups of workers chosen by us offer a useful basis for the study of the process where orientations toward work are related to and developed within the structure of a specific work situation. It is clear that they did form real groups with certain distinctive characteristics and the members of each aware of their being different from the other three groups. It has also shown, however, that the categories we have employed are – like so many of the categories used by sociologists – to some extent arbitrary, quite important variations existing within each of the four groups. While we have used the four categories as the basic means of systematising the data that we have collected, we have continually been aware of other possible ways of differentiating the workforce at Brompton. In the pages that follow we have attempted to develop these alternative patterns wherever they appear appropriate.

3 The worker and the firm

When we analyse the firm as an organisation, we can do so at various levels of abstraction. We can consider it as a unit within a system of production that offers its workers wages, some security and fringe benefits, in exchange for a period of time spent working in the factory. At another level it can be analysed in terms of the social relationships that ensue between workers, and between workers and other grades in the organisation, as a result of the productive process. There is ample evidence to indicate that the workers themselves distinguish between these two levels, and that their appraisal of one may differ greatly from their appraisal of the other. In this chapter we will consider the extent to which the workers at Gourmets draw this distinction, and examine the nature of their involvement in these two aspects of the organisation.

FINDING WORK

Before we consider the relationship between the worker and the firm, it would be well to look at the past employment experience of the workers in the sample. We are considering people who, at one point of time, all chose to work for the same employer, but their patterns of employment leading to that point were widely different. The range of ages meant that they had been in the labour market for differing periods of time, quite apart from the varying types of work they had done, and of course some had been with Gourmets longer than others. For some this was the first job after leaving school while others came after doing a variety of jobs, and quite a number had suffered at least one spell of unemployment. There were, nevertheless, some important similarities.

Probably the most useful single indication of past work experience is their employment situation immediately prior to joining the firm, and this is set out in table 3.1. Many of the workers were unemployed just before joining Gourmets but in no case was this for an extended period, and the last job is recorded here. However, the experience of unemployment had influenced perceptions, as will become apparent.

A quarter of the day-shift men were school leavers compared with only one man on the night shift (who has been put in this group since it was his first job although he actually joined the firm after failing his final examinations at a College of Education), and retail work tends to be a more dominant prior occupation on the night shift (26%) than on the day shift (12%). Apart from this the immediate employment background of both groups of men appears similar.

Table 3.1   *The immediate prior employment situation of the sample members*

Job type	Day men	Night men	Full-time women	Part-time women	All
Housewife	–	–	12	37	49
School	16	1	14	–	31
Retail work	8	12	41	12	73
Unskilled manual	16	16	17	17	66
Semi-skilled manual	7	7	3	–	17
Skilled manual	8	3	1	2	14
Clerical	6	6	19	5	36
Other	3	1	2	5	11
Total	64	46	109	78	297

The fundamental differences between the two groups of women related to family background. Almost half the part-time women were full-time housewives before they came to Gourmets, and none had just left school. On the other hand 13% of the full-time women were school-leavers which was slightly more than the number who were housewives. Those part-time women who had been in employment previously were mainly in retail work (15%) or unskilled manual work (22%) of various types, particularly school cleaning⁣ and the school meals service. Among the full-time women, half of those who had been at work were in retail employment while the rest were more or less evenly divided between clerical and manual work. Like the part-time employees, few of those who came from manual jobs had had experience of large-scale factory production. Most had come from a small garment factory in the neighbouring town, from even smaller embroidery establishments or from the school meals service.

The outstanding feature of the information on previous employment is that most of the labour force came with little or no experience of work in a large factory. Well over 80% of the women in the sample had never worked inside a factory before, and although the trend is much less obvious among the men, many of them were recruited from school-leavers, retail workers or workers in building and related industries. We would expect, therefore, that this would be an important influence upon the worker's assessment of the firm, and on his or her adaptation to the job. Indeed the difficulties of adjustment were reflected in the almost universal criticism of the firm's training scheme. Management were not unaware of the problem, but the workers were generally agreed that the scheme was inadequate. Of course this does not mean that the workers were unable to adapt, but their initial experiences may have had a more lasting effect in colouring their perceptions of the firm.

Let us now consider these perceptions in some detail, starting with reasons for choosing the firm, as recalled at the time of interview.

Table 3.2   *Reasons for choosing Gourmets as a place of work (men)*

Reason	Day men		Night men		All men	
	No.	%	No.	%	No.	%
Good pay	11	17	12	26	23	21
Security	2	3	6	13	8	7
Hours	1	1	4	9	5	5
Friends worked there	25	39	6	13	31	28
Unemployed	27	42	25	54	52	47
Near home	30	47	15	33	45	41
Other	7	11	4	9	11	10
Total	103	161	72	157	175	159

* In this table and similar tables through the report, a maximum of two responses was allowed each interviewee. On no occasion did all respondents quote two reasons. In all such tables, therefore, the *actual* number of responses will be well below the maximum number. The percentage of respondents giving each response is also recorded. These percentages similarly run to less than the possible maximum of 200. The respondents were not asked to grade the importance of each reason, and we have treated each quoted response as an independent statistic. Where relationships appear to exist between first and second responses we will note them.

A first point to note is that both tables 3.2 and 3.3 (page 43) have an extremely high percentage of responses. This, as we shall see later, is rarely the case, and suggests that the workers were well aware of their reasons for beginning work with Gourmets.

If we consider the firm as an organisation that employs labour in return for certain production services, we may well expect that the worker, in assessing his employment situation, would consider the wages, hours, etc. which might be obtained at an alternative firm. Looked at from this standpoint, table 3.2 is quite surprising, as only 22% of the men (13% of the responses) on the day shift indicated pay, security or hours as an important reason for their move to Gourmets. The men on night shift, probably as a result of their previous unemployment and size of families, were more likely to have been attracted by the economic aspects of the firm than the men on the day shift.

The overriding determinant behind the choice of Gourmets by the men appears to be that they were unemployed and/or that the firm was near at hand.

'I was made redundant. I tried a couple of places. Gourmets were advertising — and Browns were — at the time. I could have gone to Browns — a few of my mates were there — but I'd have had to travel across the city. It puts hours on the day. Gourmets are on my door step by comparison.'

'I was made unemployed at my old place. It was a bad job anyway — they messed you about — and a lot of us were laid off at the same time. A few of my mates came here — *they* were recruiting at the Labour — so I came along. It's a job.'

'I was travelling about two and a half hours a day when I was at Wilson's. The money was alright, but it was wearing me out. Gourmets were advertising in the Evening Post so I thought I'd give it a try. I can walk to work now.'

'I was unemployed. I knew I could get a job here — they were always advertising. I thought of it as a temporary affair until I got back on my feet.'

The existence of a high level of unemployment in the area exerted an overwhelming influence upon the occupational choices of workers — 47% of the men in our sample had been unemployed before coming to Gourmets and most of them mentioned this as the main reason behind their decision to work there. The considerations of the unemployed were undoubtedly economic, but here the prime concern was obtaining work rather than the level of return. A higher proportion of the night men gave this reason while the day men were more likely to be influenced by the convenience of work near home.[1]

Friendship links appear to have played an important role on the day shift, 39% of the men pointing to this as a reason. Its greater importance among the day men can partly be explained by the fact that school-leavers are more likely to be influenced by where their friends work than are middle-aged men, although the night men were generally less interested in friendships, as we shall see. However, it should also be noted that fifteen of the twenty-five responses that quoted the 'friendship system' were given as second responses in conjunction with either 'unemployment' or 'convenience' as a first response.

Similar information for the women is shown in table 3.3. The pattern here is slightly different from that shown in table 3.2. Among the full-time women marginally more moved to Gourmets after an appraisal of the comparative level of pay than in any other group. This, like the similar choices of men on night shift, can be explained by the low level of pay that they were receiving

Table 3.3   *Reasons for choosing Gourmets as a place of work (women)**

Reason	Full-time women		Part-time women		All women	
	No.	%	No.	%	No.	%
Good pay	32	29	3	4	35	19
Security	2	2	–	–	2	1
Hours	11	10	24	31	35	19
Friends worked there	36	33	20	26	56	30
Unemployed	13	12	6	8	19	10
Near home	40	37	21	27	61	33
Lonely at home	20	18	36	46	56	30
Needed extra money	5	5	36	46	41	22
Other	24	22	7	9	31	17
Total	183	168	153	193	333	180

* Two responses were allowed; see note to table 3.2.

1 While consistent with the trend on other reasons, the difference between shifts on these two reasons was not significant.

in their retail or clerical jobs. The part-time women were the group most concerned about the hours of work. Family responsibilities make convenient working hours essential for these women and as a result nearly a third quoted favourable hours as the main reason behind their choice of Gourmets. Like the men, an appreciable number of women in each group stressed the importance of proximity and friends, although this was more frequent among the full-time women.

The situation is complicated by the fact that the part-time women were also housewives. Loneliness while the children were at school, and the need for extra money were frequently mentioned by this group. Each reason was given by nearly half of the women in this group and many gave both, sometimes explicitly indicating their decision was based on a combination of the two.

'The children were at school and I had a lot of time on my hands. The main problem was the money though. We were *really* short of extras. Heaps of women on the estate worked here so I knew that it wasn't heavy work. So I just applied.'

'I've always worked — up until I had the children that is. I used to like working with a lot of people. Have a laugh. When the children went to school I got a job in a shop. I didn't like it that much, and I wanted Saturdays off. I missed factory life and Gourmets were advertising at the time so I applied.'

'We wanted to keep the children at school. They're all at the Grammar school. We'd just moved to Brompton so the children had to have school dinners anyway; so I thought I'd get a job. *He* didn't like the idea at first but I talked him round. Our next-door neighbour was here and that helped. The hours were good. I could get everything done at home in the afternoon.'

'I was working in a shop and it shut down. We relied upon the money so I applied for a job here. I started the week after.'

In a sense their responses are not comparable to the others, being the reasons for taking employment at all rather than choosing a particular employer. They clearly indicate, however, the significance of work in the lives of these women and also that Gourmets provided an employment opportunity for them which, to a large extent, was not otherwise available. The part-time women were more conscious than any other group of their relationship with the labour market because their position was much more tentative. In making the decision to begin work again, hours of work and payment had to be considered closely and discussed with their husbands who in many instances were initially antagonistic to their plans.

In summary, it would appear that the proximity of the factory to the homes of potential workers was a prime determinant in their selection of Gourmets. This choice was assisted by the low level of wages and the high rate of unemployment in the area, and was further influenced by the 'friendship system', and the convenient hours offered by the firm for women wanting part-time work. Although there appeared to have been little conscious assessment of the actual employment situation at Gourmets, we would expect the firm's local 'image' to have influenced decisions. It is probable that within any particular locality workers, through conversations with their friends and workmates, develop 'images of firms' in the area which they bring into play when they consider changing jobs. At Brompton, Gourmets seems to be thought of as a reasonably good employer paying relatively high wages.

ASSESSMENT OF THE FIRM

When respondents were asked to compare Gourmets with other firms of which they had had experience, it soon became obvious that the question was rather meaningless to many of them, as they had little basis for comparison. As, however, we were interested in the perception which the workers had of the firm rather than objective comparisons, where respondents had little or no comparable work experience we asked them how they thought the firm compared with the other employers in the area. The general consensus in all groups was that Gourmets was at least an average firm. Indeed about half of

Table 3.4 *How does Gourmets compare with other firms of which you have had experience?*

	Day men	Night men	Full-time women	Part-time women	All
The best	4	2	9	7	22
One of the best	19	20	39	33	111
Average	34	21	56	33	144
One of the worst	5	2	2	2	11
Worst	–	–	3	1	4
No response	2	1	–	2	5
Total	64	46	109	78	297

the night men and the part-time women rated the firm higher than average, while 36% and 44% of the day men and full-time women did the same. On the other hand only about 8% of the day men and 4% of other workers rated the firm below average.

Attractions

This information in itself is not very useful or illuminating. It tells us merely that most of the workers at Brompton did not feel that there were factory jobs near at hand that were far superior to their own. Such a view could coexist with a variety of different interpretations of one's position in the market for labour and it is obviously necessary to enquire further into the reasoning that supported such an assessment of Gourmets. During the interview each worker was asked what he considered to be the best thing about the Company. Their answers were categorised and are presented in table 3.5, again allowing up to two responses from each person. An initial comment on table 3.5 is that the response level is much lower than in tables 3.2 and 3.3. The part-time women were much more prone to give two responses (56%) than the other groups, while at the other extreme only 27% of the day men gave more than one response.

No-one who has travelled in the bus from Brompton at the end of a shift can doubt that the women develop friendship links with their workmates. So it is not surprising that many of them (40% of full-time women and 42% of part-time workers) saw the atmosphere on the shop floor as being the most likeable thing about the firm. This was by far the most frequent response of the women yet was rarely mentioned by the men and then almost entirely on the day shift.[2] However, it can be too easily assumed that these relationships in themselves are enough to make the women satisfied with their jobs. It should be appreciated that over half the women did not mention this factor and that many women mentioned other factors − particularly rates of pay, hours and conditions − either to the exclusion of or together with the social atmosphere.

Several referred to what we have termed the 'ethos' of the firm − the general atmosphere, resulting more from the attitudes of top management rather than of workmates, but even if we add these to the more explicit references to atmosphere they still only account for just over half the respondents and 39% of responses; an impressively high but not overwhelming frequency.

---

2 Each group of women gave this response significantly more often than the day men, who in turn gave it significantly more than the night shift.

Table 3.5 *The best thing about Gourmets**

Response	Day men		Night men		Full-time women		Part time women		All	
	No.	%	No.	%	No.	%	No.	%	No.	%
Pay	3	5	6	13	21	19	17	22	47	16
Hours	10	16	20	43	23	21	22	28	75	25
Security	2	3	6	13	1	1	–	–	9	3
Fringe benefits	1	2	10	22	3	3	2	3	16	5
Working conditions	4	6	6	13	11	10	12	15	33	11
Near home	11	17	3	7	7	6	8	10	29	10
Social facilities	16	25	1	2	8	7	6	8	31	10
Atmosphere	12	19	1	2	44	40	33	42	90	30
'Ethos' of the firm	8	13	4	9	17	16	9	12	38	13
Other	3	5	3	7	1	1	9	12	16	5
Nothing	11	17	5	11	7	6	3	4	26	9
Total	81	127	65	141	143	131	121	155	410	138

* Two responses were allowed, see note to table 3.2.

The two groups of men present greatly different conceptions of the best thing about the firm. The night men continually referred to what may, in a general way, be termed the 'primary economic' features of their employment situation. Pay and security were not referred to particularly often, although together they amounted for 18% of the responses. Fringe benefits were mentioned 15% of the time, and working conditions 9%. The most frequent replies, however, were related to hours, the attraction being the night shift system which gave a long weekend off work. This represented a further 31% of the responses. Nearly all gave at least one of these reasons, apart from five dissatisfied men who could think of nothing they liked best. In sharp contrast to this, the men on day shift, save for the 12% of responses that mention the hours of work, tended to rate highly variables other than the primary economic ones. The social facilities and atmosphere on the shop floor received 20% and 15% of the responses respectively, while 'proximity to home' got eleven mentions (14%). The proportions of the men giving each type of response were 25%, 19% and 17%, but several men gave more than one so that a little over half the men gave one or more of these responses. This was also the group with the highest proportion who said there was nothing they liked best.

Much of the difference between the day and the night shifts can be explained by the fact that the shifts were being asked to rate different work situations. The hours and wages on night shift are obviously different from day shift, as is the night-shift men's ability to enjoy the social facilities. Nevertheless, security of employment and fringe benefits are constant for both shifts, but the night shift rated them much more frequently.

In explaining these variations it will be useful to consider the differing orientations to work of the men on the day and night shifts. These orientations, we have argued, will vary with age and family responsibilities and so it is significant that the frequency with which 'security of employment' and 'fringe benefits' were quoted increased progressively with the age of the respondents, being particularly marked among those over 50. The responses of the day men, taken by themselves, were too few to argue a trend but among the night men it was clearly significant. This finding is not surprising, given that many of these men were of an age when pensions loom important and getting another job might be difficult. In our society manual workers who approach retirement age become increasingly vulnerable and this fact is clearly demonstrated by the men on the night shift. For young men, however, the situation is far less pressing and consequently the concern for security among the night men contrasts with the emphasis placed upon social facilities and friendships within the day shift.

There was an overwhelming tendency for these answers referring to 'social'

Table 3.6　*The relationship between age and assessment of the firm:*
　　　　　day men's responses (social factors)

Best thing about Gourmets	Age			All
	Under 20	20-29	30+	
Social facilities	9	7	–	16
Atmosphere	6	3	3	12
Other	6	15	32	53
Total responses	21	25	35	81
Respondents	17	17	30	64

aspects of the firm to come from the younger men, as table 3.6 shows. About 90% of respondents under 20 years gave one of these responses. The tendency is particularly marked with reference to the social facilities. This probably reflects the younger men's greater participation in sports, but also the greater opportunity and interest of those without family ties; of the sixteen mentioning social facilities fourteen were unmarried and another had no children.

As we noted with regard to the women and the friendly social atmosphere, we should be wary of assuming that social facilities and good workmates are sufficient, in themselves, to provide young men with a satisfying job. In fact it may well be that the excessive reliance placed by the men of the day shift upon social variables, and proximity to home, to the exclusion of primary economic ones can be taken as an indicator of discontent among the group. It should be noted that 17% of the men on day shift were unable to see anything that was best about Gourmets. Satisfaction or discontent depends also on what workers expect from an employer, and in this respect social factors were not prominent. We shall be able to give a closer examination of this when we have developed the theme further.

Disadvantages

At this point in the argument we must revert back to the two levels of analysis of the firm to which we referred earlier. In table 3.5, particularly among the night men, it was seen that the firm was primarily appraised as an

Table 3.7 *The worst thing about Gourmets**

Response	Day men		Night men		Full-time women		Part-time women		All	
	No.	%	No.	%	No.	%	No.	%	No.	%
Pay	1	2	3	7	–	–	4	5	8	3
Hours	–	–	1	2	4	4	3	4	8	3
Promotion	4	6	3	7	2	2	1	1	10	3
Working condition	1	2	–	–	7	6	13	17	21	7
Payment system	11	17	7	15	6	6	8	10	32	11
Type of work	4	6	9	20	21	19	13	17	47	16
Organisation of work	6	9	16	35	21	19	16	21	59	20
Rules	2	3	2	4	13	12	8	10	25	8
Supervision	19	30	7	15	31	28	6	8	63	21
'Ethos' of the firm	5	8	2	4	6	6	–	–	13	4
Other	3	5	–	–	5	5	10	13	18	6
Nothing	17	27	9	20	26	24	20	26	72	24
Total	73	114	59	128	142	130	102	131	376	127

* Two responses were allowed, see note to table 3.2.

economic organisation, while the features of the firm on the shop floor were mentioned only by reference to 'working conditions' and 'atmosphere on the shop floor'. In table 3.7, however, this latter trend has been widely developed. In assessing the worst thing about the firm the worker is basically critical of the firm as it affects him while he works. The features of the firm that he dislikes most are those which impede his action in the work situation – the control system. Although one or two workers did see the level of pay or length of hours as the worst thing about the firm, in general criticism was based upon aspects of the workers' shop floor relationships.

The 'type of work' and 'organisation of work' were quoted with equal regularity by part-time and full-time groups of women. For the part-time workers, the casual nature of their work when they were without a permanent job appeared as a source of considerable distress. One of them particularly disliked having to stand outside the supervisor's office, which she likened to a cattle auction. Of more general concern, however, was the loss of friendly relationships in a stable work group. 'Rules and regulations' were objected to more or less equally by both groups of women. Difficulties associated with leaving the job to go to the toilet appeared often as a source of annoyance, while having to clock out on leaving the department, and the no-smoking rule were all frequently criticised.

In contrast to the men, a number of women, especially the part-time workers, were critical of working conditions. It is of interest to note that all of the twenty women who rated the working conditions as the worst thing were married. Dirty or cracked cups were one specific reason for complaint. The full-time women, however, were much more prone to find reason for complaint in the supervision. This was the fault they referred to most often, and they were far more conscious of supervisory controls. The fact that most members of this group belonged to a different generation from their supervisors is probably important here, as older women on both shifts were less likely to give this response.

Among the men, type and organisation of work and supervision were again principle causes of complaint, but there were interesting differences between shifts. The night men were like the women in referring to the type of work and its organisation; indeed they gave these responses a little more frequently. On the other hand the day men did not give these answers very often but were just as likely as the full-time women to complain of supervision. It is worth recalling that the night men were doing much the same work as the women – essentially machine-paced conveyor-belt work – whereas the day men were not. Thus we might expect the technological similarity of job content to lead to similar evaluation of the work from the night men and the women, in spite of the social factors producing different attitudes to most aspects of their employment.[3] The day men resembled the full-time women in being generally younger than their supervisors, and amongst the men the unfavourable references to supervision came predominantly from the younger workers, including over half those under 20.

The remaining feature named with any frequency as the worst thing about the firm was the payment system. To understand this it must be realised that the firm had recently changed from a system which many workers did not understand to a new system which even more workers did not understand. We shall return to this later on. It may be that the workers would come to understand the system better in time. If so, the responses reflected a passing cause of annoyance, but as we shall see, incomprehensible payments had become part of the folklore of the factory.

Finally we should note that there were significantly less responses naming the worst thing than there were for the best thing. Less gave two answers and more said nothing.[4] This can be taken as some indication of general satisfaction with the firm. The contrast was greatest among the part-time women.

When asked what things needed changing at Gourmets about a quarter, though rather less of the night men, replied 'nothing'. For the rest, the trend of criticism revealed in table 3.7 continued. The members of the sample, logically enough, wished to change those things which they thought worst about the firm. However, answers to this type of question also depend on what changes the respondent conceives to be structurally feasible. Thus it is interesting to note that not one of the thirty-five[5] who regarded the type of work as the worst thing about the firm thought it relevant to suggest that it needed changing. This seems to imply an acceptance of the type of work as a given which cannot be changed. The only other significant change from table 3.7 was a decline from 30% to 13% in the number of day men saying supervision and an increase in those referring to organisation of work, thus making their answers similar to those of the night men. It is possible that the explanation is much the same, the men seeing it as easier to change the work organisation than the people who supervise it, but this is not clear.

---

3 See Blauner, *Alienation and Freedom*; Woodward, *Industrial Organisation*. It is possible that the slightly higher tendency of the night men to give these responses reflects a tendency to view the work as 'women's work' and so somewhat distasteful.
4 The trend was observed in all groups, though not always significant. The trend for the total sample was highly significant.
5 Unadjusted figures, i.e. actual respondents.

Commitment to the firm

Finally, on this theme, we asked respondents how they would feel if, for some reason, they had to leave Gourmets and work for another firm in the area, for much the same pay and conditions. It was hoped that this question would reveal the extent to which the worker had become involved in the firm, beyond the level of his work role. The results are analysed in tables 3.8 and 3.9.

Table 3.8   *How respondents would feel if they had to leave Gourmets*

	Day men	Night men	Full-time women	Part-time women	All
Very badly	8	15	30	22	75
Quite badly	15	9	22	19	65
Wouldn't mind all that much	16	10	28	26	80
Wouldn't mind at all	19	12	24	10	65
Be pleased	6	–	5	1	12
Total	64	46	109	78	297

Roughly half of the women and the night men, but only 36% of the day men recorded that they would feel badly or very badly because of the move. On the other hand the day men were more likely to say they would be pleased or would not mind at all. Here again is an indication of lower commitment and satisfaction among the day men. It is interesting that twelve people said that they would be pleased to move. The explanation of this lies in the fact that, apart from one part-time woman who was about to leave anyway, the workers who gave this response were all under 25 and all badly wanted to be doing a 'better job'. Typical responses here were:

A 17-year-old lad who 'serviced' belts in one of the big departments:
> 'This job just doesn't seem important to me at all. There doesn't seem any achievement. I don't want a fantastic career but I'd like to get something done. I feel like I'm dying here; smothering or something.'

A girl on a packing belt in Big Block:
> 'Yes I'd be pleased if this place closed down. I'd *have* to go then. I hate this job, but I just can't get round to leaving. I'd really like to do

53

something that is interesting. You'd need qualifications I suppose though — you'd have to go to night school.'

Table 3.9   *Reasons for responses in table 3.8*

Feel badly because:

	Day men	Night men	Full-time women	Part-time women	All
Miss friends	14	2	46	33	95
Travel to work	7	6	2	5	20
Miss security	–	13	4	3	20
'Good firm'	2	3	–	–	5
Total	23	24	52	41	140

Not feel badly because:

	Day men	Night men	Full-time women	Part-time women	All
All jobs are the same	12	10	33	18	73
– *But* miss friends	2	5	18	12	37
Want better job	27	7	6	7	47
Total	41	22	57	37	157

Looking generally at the reasons for their answers, we can see that, apart from those factors specifically excluded — the pay and conditions — the predominant link with the firm for the women was the friendship group. The vast majority of those who would feel badly about leaving gave the loss of friends as the major reason. Even of those women who wouldn't mind the move, almost a third remarked (unprompted) that they would miss their friends.

For the men the patterns of reasons are rather different. Among the day men who would feel badly if they left, the loss of friends figures as the most important single reason, though not so strikingly as among the women. The salient feature of this group, however, is the high percentage of respondents who expressed dissatisfaction with their jobs; 42% of them saw their jobs as inferior to alternative occupations, while a further 22% saw them as no worse but certainly not better.

The night shift presents a completely different picture. Here commitment to the firm was greater, and about a third said they would feel very badly, which is more than in any of the other groups.[6] Although loss of friends played some part in enforcing this commitment, the main reasons are seen to be 'primary economic' in nature, even when pay itself is excluded. The security offered by Gourmets was seen as important by this group, and it is the prospect of its loss that bound them to the firm. As one 45-year-old packing belt worker put it:

'I would hate to have to leave here now; at my age. It's not a great job but it's given me something that I've never had. I know that I can stay here till I retire or drop dead. At my age with the kids that's important. I don't want any dole.'

PERCEPTIONS OF MANAGEMENT

So far we have observed that the workers were, in general, satisfied with the basic 'economic' benefits that they received from the firm, and that their criticism tended to centre around the control system: i.e. on the way in which the firm's policies affected the employee at work. In the following paragraphs we will briefly consider the extent to which this two tier analysis affected the workers' perceptions of 'management'. In each of the questions respondents were asked to think of management as above the level of department manager.

When asked whether they thought the fact that Gourmets was a family firm made any difference to the employees, over a quarter of the day men were unable to comprehend the question. A further 32% of them thought it made no difference while 61% of the night shift, 55% of the full-time women, and 37% of the part-time women gave similar responses. The women were much more inclined than the men to see the 'family firm' in a favourable light. While a few of the men on nights claimed that they were not allowed a licensed club because of the values of the owning family, no women voiced any points of criticism. In fact 16% of the full-time women and 31% of the part-time women thought that family ownership resulted in a greater interest being taken in the employees. Examples of how the firm had been understanding during periods of family difficulty were frequent from the part-time women. An interesting point to note, finally, is that 8% of the full-time women and smaller proportions of other groups insisted that the

---

6 Although the difference from the groups of women is not significant.

family were all right but that 'it's the people inside that spoil it'. These respondents left the interviewer in no doubt that 'the people' being referred to were the supervisory staff. Here again we see an example of the individual worker distinguishing between 'the firm' and his or her work experience. Frequently throughout the interview respondents professed the belief that 'they (the family) can't know that's going on, or else they'd stop it'. On as many occasions the interviewer was taken for an emissary who would communicate their misgivings and problems to the 'higher-ups'.[7]

In order to explore further the way in which workers at Brompton perceived the position of management in the factory, each respondent was asked whether he or she agreed with a series of statements relating to management. From these it emerged that, in general, they considered that management had a difficult job to do — more difficult than many people think, according to 80% of the respondents. Also, as table 3.10 shows, they were reluctant to suggest that the managers were paid too much.

Table 3.10 *'Management at Gourmets are paid too much'*

	Day men	Night men	Full-time women	Part-time women	All
Agree	13	2	28	6	49
Disagree	10	9	17	8	44
Don't know	41	35	64	64	204
Total	64	46	109	78	297

Of interest here is the high number of respondents who recorded 'don't know'. It appears to be a further indication of the social and physical distance that the workers see to be between them and the higher levels of administration. This was substantiated by the responses to a direct question whether the management of the firm were out of touch with the feelings of the workers. About two-thirds thought management were out of touch with their immediate problems on the shop floor. This gives us a further indication of the worker's double analysis of the firm. While he, in general, approved of the 'firm', he felt himself isolated in the work situation and left to the vagaries of the illegitimate powers of the various control systems on the shop

---

7 Similar attitudes have been found in other studies, e.g. Liverpool University Department of Social Science, *The Dock Worker.*

floor. We will return to this problem later; at the moment let us take a closer look at the worker's perception of the manager's role. Table 3.10 shows that among the workers who did express an opinion about whether their managers were paid too much, there were differences between groups. The two groups who generally tended to be more well disposed to the firm — the night men and part-time women — were more likely to deny that management were paid too much. On the other hand the day men and full-time women more often thought the managers were overpaid. A similar trend was also revealed on the question whether management were out of touch with the workers, the part-time women and night men being less apt to be critical.

Table 3.11 *'The management at Gourmets are genuinely interested in the well-being of the workers'*

	Day men	Night men	Full-time women	Part-time women	All
Agree	38	29	71	66	204
Disagree	26	17	33	8	84
Don't know	–	–	5	4	9
Total	64	46	109	78	297

In spite of the belief that managers were out of touch, all groups tended to agree that the management were genuinely interested in the well-being of the workers (table 3.11). However, they agreed with differing degrees of certainty, with the part-time women much more sure than any other group. Frequency of agreement ranged from 87% of the part-time women down to 59% of the day men. An interesting feature of the day men's responses is their variation by department; in the larger departments, where their work was integrated with that of the women, over 70% of the men agreed with the statement, while 64% of the men in smaller departments, who were relatively isolated, disagreed.

If the perceptions of management so far presented seem somewhat confused, then confusion is confounded when we see that the majority of workers also agreed with the statement that, given the chance, the management would 'put one over' on the workers.

All but the part-time women, and they with less conviction than previously, seem to have given responses that are directly opposed to those

57

Table 3.12 *'Given the chance the management at Gourmets would put one over on the workers'*

	Day men	Night men	Full-time women	Part-time women	All
Agree	49	30	70	27	176
Disagree	14	15	34	44	107
Don't know	1	1	5	7	14
Total	64	46	109	78	297

they presented in table 3.11.[8] This may possibly be explained by the fact that people are more prone to agree than disagree with anything, especially if their involvement is low, but this seems unlikely to account for such a contrast. A far more likely reason is that the workers perceive 'putting one over on them whenever possible' to be an accepted feature of the managerial role, and within this they will attend to the workers' well-being whenever it is feasible to do so. 'Putting one over' is part of the impersonal structural conflict of interest inherent in the firm, while concern for the workers' well-being – even by a management who is out of touch – is at the level of personal relations.

It is worth noting that the part-time women, in their consistently sympathetic perception of the managerial role, were atypical of the workforce at large. An explanation for this can probably be found in their shorter periods of time at the factory and, more importantly, their related family roles. They were less likely to be 'work orientated' than any other group, and yet they were more likely to have sought, and obtained, the help of the firm in times of family difficulty. Also they were working hours which had been designed to attract, and thus to meet the needs of married women. These factors combined to differentiate them from the other workers in their attitudes toward management.

Finally, let us look briefly at attitudes to the welfare schemes, since the firm, maintaining the Gourmet tradition, attached considerable importance to the provision of good schemes. In fact the workers did tend to be appreciative of the schemes. However, nearly a quarter of the men on days and as many as two-thirds of the part-time women professed ignorance of all the schemes. This ignorance among the part-time women is not surprising in view of their

8 Of course, some of the individual respondents were consistent in adopting a sympathetic or hostile view of management, but many were not.

low commitment to work. The large proportion of the day men claiming ignorance is further indication of the low level of involvement among this group.

SUMMARY

Most of the sample came to Gourmets with an employment background vitally different from the experience of a large factory, and large batch production. This led to problems of adapting to the new work environment, as was apparent from criticisms of the training scheme. Nevertheless, they tended to rate Gourmets quite highly as a firm — at least average, and much above average for many people,[9] although they voiced a fair number of criticisms. The men on day shift, and to some extent the full-time women, were less enamoured of the place.

An important reason for many of the workers coming to the factory in the first place was its proximity to their homes. This, together with low wages in alternative occupations and convenient hours for the women, resulted in Gourmets being chosen. Unemployment for the men, family budget problems and loneliness at home among married women made the opportunity to work at Gourmets welcome.

The women were much more likely to think that the family ownership of the firm resulted in a greater interest being taken by the firm in employees. All groups, although sections of the day shift were exceptions, saw management as interested in the well being of the employees. At the same time it was generally regarded as part of their role to 'put one over on the workers'. The part-time women were exceptional in being the only group which tended to have consistently sympathetic perceptions of management.

The night men were most likely to consider important, and to value highly, the basic economic features of employment. In describing the best thing about the firm a surprisingly large number referred to the hours, with the remaining responses centring round fringe benefits, pay, security and conditions. In contrast the day men, particularly the young men, were more appreciative of the leisure facilities and social aspects of their employment.

The women attached importance to the basic features of their employment, and the pay, hours and conditions were frequently mentioned as the best things about the firm. However, the friendship pattern on the shop floor was *the* most attractive feature of the firm. In evaluating highly the social rewards of their work, they did not share the young men's appreciation of extra work social facilities; several mentioned relations with management,

---

9 Only 5% rated the firm below average while 45% rated it one of the best or the best firm they knew.

but it was the company of their workmates that was most important. For many, the happy relationships at work contrasted favourably with their previous loneliness at home.

In general the firm itself was seen as being a good one, and there was little dissatisfaction with wages, hours or security. However, there appeared to be a strong undercurrent of discontent that was mainly associated with the organisation of work as it affected respondents in their work roles. This appeared to run throughout the factory, but to take on a different form with each group. In particular we noted that those employed on the main mass-production jobs (night men and the women) were liable to complain about the type and organisation of their work, and also the young workers of both sexes tended to be antagonistic to the supervision.

In considering perceptions of the firm, different patterns have emerged for each of the four groups. The attachment to the firm of men on the night shift was primarily instrumental and as their expectations were relatively well met they tended to be satisfied. These were predominantly married men with family responsibilities making a good steady wage important, and the experience of unemployment also added to their valuing of security. Sickness and pension schemes were similarly valued, particularly by the older men.

Of course the other workers also regarded economic factors as important but their patterns of involvement were different. The other group showing positive satisfaction was the part-time women, who were all married. The special shifts run by the firm gave them the opportunity to go out to work and bring in some extra money for the family. Beyond this their attachment to the firm was predominantly social. Their involvement in work was extremely low, and they appreciated a firm which enabled them to give priority to their roles of housewife and mother, while providing work in a friendly atmosphere.

The full-time women also valued the social rewards but were generally less satisfied. Whereas their commitment to work was greater, both because they invested more hours there and because many did not have alternative family roles for their involvement, their rewards appeared less. They had less reason to feel that Gourmets was providing employment to suit their needs, and their perceptions of the firm was generally less favourable.

However, the group with the lowest commitment to the firm were the day men. Young, irked by supervision, without the economic incentive of family dependants, their main attachment to Gourmets was social. Social facilities and friendships were the main attractions, but these were weak ties. Many were basically dissatisfied with their jobs and their attachment to the firm was minimal.

In the following chapters we shall make a closer analysis of the different patterns of involvement and the lines of inquiry suggested here.

4   The worker and his job

Following the analysis which we began in chapter 3, we intend in this chapter to examine the relationship between the worker and his work. Initially, we shall examine the expectations of the worker and compare them with his perception of the rewards in his present job. We will consider his relationship with the actual work process, and also with the workers with whom he is placed in contact by this work process. Finally we shall consider the operation of the payment system and its relation to work done, as seen by the workers.

IMPORTANT ASPECTS OF A JOB

During the interview each of the respondents was asked to rate the *importance* of a given set of job characteristics. The results of this question are shown in the following table.

Table 4.1 clearly shows that good pay and security were the most important features of a job for both groups of men. Good pay was rated 'Most important' or 'Second most important' by 52% of the day men and 59% of the men on night shift, while security scored 45% on days and 48% on nights. Following these in order of importance appear conditions of work and promotion prospects on the day shift, and convenient hours and working conditions on the night shift.

For both groups of men, easy work was the least important feature of a job, 41% of the night men and 23% of the day men mentioning it. Good social facilities also appear to have been of little importance to both groups.

These responses throw some light on our findings of the last chapter. Although day men did not have the economic pressure of the 'life-cycle squeeze' they tended to give the conventional answer in rating pay and security as most important.[1] Indeed they were more likely than the night men to give these first importance. Unlike the night men, they were unwilling, or unable because of their age to take the necessary steps to maximise their economic rewards, but they still felt them to be important. Recalling that it was not pay but social facilities − not regarded as important − which they

---

1 The family men were, in fact, more likely to stress security. Over half the married men did so, and of the eleven men with two or more children, ten referred to security.

Table 4.1 *The relative importance of various aspects of a job*

Aspects of a job	Day men			Night men			Full-time women			Part-time women		
	1st	2nd	least	1st	2nd	least	1st	2nd	least	1st	2nd	least
Good pay	22	11	–	12	15	–	10	33	–	10	11	–
Security	21	8	–	12	10	–	19	12	1	2	2	2
Good conditions	3	17	1	2	6	1	35	20	–	25	15	–
Convenient hours	1	1	1	6	2	2	7	12	1	24	19	–
Promotion opportunities	4	8	5	3	–	2	4	–	16	–	1	20
Worthwhile/interesting work	3	2	1	5	1	1	7	9	–	1	1	2
Easy to get to	2	6	4	–	4	1	7	2	7	6	7	5
Friendly workmates	1	2	4	2	2	1	12	14	5	2	12	5
Understanding supervision	1	2	–	–	1	2	5	6	1	7	7	2
Good social facilities	1	1	11	–	–	5	–	–	19	–	–	–
Good trade union branch	1	1	11	–	1	5	–	–	34	1	–	17
Good shop-steward	–	–	2	–	–	3	–	1	5	–	–	17
Work not too difficult	–	–	15	1	–	19	3	–	20	–	3	4
No response	4	5	9	3	4	4	–	–	–	–	–	9
Totals	64	64	64	46	46	46	109	109	109	78	78	78

Importance

62

saw as the firm's main attraction, we understand more clearly their low attachment to the firm.

Working conditions (rated of first or second importance by 53% of respondents), good pay (35%), security (28%) and friendly workmates (24%) were the most important features of a job for the full-time women. The part-time women also rated conditions of work (51%) and good pay (27%) highly, followed by friendly workmates and understanding supervisors (each 18%), but gave little importance to security. On the other hand they gave highest priority to convenient working hours (55%). The pattern is much as we would expect in view of our earlier discussion, although we might have anticipated rather more importance being attached to friendly workmates. Of course understanding supervision also contributes to a friendly atmosphere, but it seems that although the friendly atmosphere at Gourmets was highly valued, it was not generally regarded as an essential part of the job. The importance of hours to those with home responsibilities shows up not only in the priorities of the part-time women but also in a tendency among the full-time women for those mentioning hours to be the married women, particularly those with children. The lower importance attached to security by the women, especially the part-time workers, reflects the fact that a woman in our society is rarely the main breadwinner for a family. The married women were probably more concerned about their husbands' security, and the single women were likely to become married.[2]

As in the case of the men, both groups of women saw easy work and good social facilities among the least important things in a job. The situation is complicated, however, by the fact that the women also rated 'promotion opportunities' low down on the list — 13% of the full-time and 26% of the part-time mentioned this — together with a 'good trade union branch' which received 31% of the full-time womens' and 22% of the part-time womens' responses. Here again, particularly with regard to promotion, we have an indication of low commitment to work.

EXPECTATIONS AND SATISFACTION

Let us now compare what the worker expected from a job with what he saw his present job providing. It is to be expected that any discrepancy between the workers' expectations and their actual rewards would result in strain and discontent. Table 4.2 on p. 65 presents the things the men in the sample considered to be best catered for, and worst catered for, in their present jobs.

---

2 The part-time women were all married, and among the full-time women there was a tendency for those who were married to rate security less often, though this was not significant.

It should be borne in mind throughout the following analysis that there is inevitably a 'feed back' component in all these responses. For example, people are more likely to be conscious of any shortcomings in the things that are important to them, and are thus more prone to give critical responses. Conversely they are more likely to give importance to things they feel deficient. Thus, the more important their work is to them, the more critical are they likely to be. So, because of their greater commitment to work through economic necessity (and social convention of the man being the 'breadwinner'), we would expect men to be more critical than women. Similarly, other things being equal we would expect full-time women to be more critical than part-time women and probably the family men of the night shift to be more critical than their day time counterparts with less responsibilities. Also if there were any particular aspect of their work which was especially unsatisfactory its importance is likely to have been somewhat overemphasised, thus exaggerating overall discontent. These reservations must be kept in mind in making any comparisons between our groups of workers.

Best and worst aspects of the job

The night men saw security (28%), 'easy to get to' (15%), convenient hours (11%) and friendly workmates (11%) as being the best things about their jobs. It is interesting to note that two of these — security and hours — were rated earlier as being very important features of a job for these men. This initial analysis suggests that they saw their jobs satisfying basic expectations, but we must return to this point presently for closer examination. Worthwhile work (22%) and promotion prospects (20%) were seen as the things which were worst catered for on the night shift. In chapter 3 we saw that this group consistently rated type and organisation of work among the worst features of the firm. It seems that although a large proportion of this group may have been contented with the basic economic rewards of the job, a considerable area of potential conflict was associated with the controls exercised over the worker in the work situation. We will consider this in more detail later in the chapter.

The men on day shift rated the 'work not too difficult' (20%), 'easy to get to' (20%), friendly workmates (14%) and convenient hours (9%) as the things best catered for in their jobs. None of these was frequently rated among the two most important things in a job; in fact easy work was consistently rated among the least important things for the men in this group. There is indication here, therefore, of considerable tension, and this becomes clearer when we see that three of the things rated frequently as the worst catered for — promotion (14%), conditions of work (12%) and good pay (8%) — were listed among the four most important things for this group. An additional 14% of the group felt that their work was not worthwhile. Taken together, and remembering the conclusions in the last chapter, these responses seem to indicate that this group as a whole manifested a degree of dissatisfaction with their jobs which was atypical of the factory.

Table 4.2   *Relative appraisal of aspects of present job (men)*

	Day men		Night men	
	Best catered for	Worst catered for	Best catered for	Worst catered for
Good pay	1	5	2	2
Security of employment	3	1	13	–
Working conditions	5	8	3	3
Convenient hours	6	1	5	–
Promotion opportunities	2	9	–	9
Worthwhile/interesting work	–	9	–	10
Easy to get to	13	1	7	–
Friendly workmates	9	–	5	–
Understanding supervision	–	4	1	3
Social facilities	–	2	–	2
Trade union branch	–	4	–	3
Shop-steward	–	2	–	–
Work not too difficult	13	2	1	–
No response	12	16	9	14
Total	64	64	46	46

The full-time women saw good pay (19%), easy work (16%), friendly workmates (16%) and good working conditions (15%) as the things best catered for in their jobs. Apart from easy work, these were among the things most often mentioned as important in a job in table 4.1. Promotion opportunities, supervision, type of work and the trade union branch were seen as being the things worst catered for in their jobs. Two of these – promotion opportunities and trade union branch – were rated consistently as the least important features of the job by this group. We should note that they all relate to aspects of control which we discussed in chapter 1. Although these are not listed among the primary expectations of this group, which appear to have been fairly well satisfied by the firm, they may well indicate an area of secondary expectations which were not being fulfilled.

Unlike any other group the part-time women stressed the convenience of the hours as the thing that was best catered for in their jobs. Twenty-eight per cent of them quoted this, and it was this that they saw to be the most important thing for them in a job. Easy work (18%) and good working conditions (10%) were also mentioned with some frequency. As the latter was also mentioned as an important feature of a job, we would expect that this group of women found their basic job expectations satisfied at Gourmets.

Table 4.3   *The relative appraisal of various aspects of present job (women)*

	Full-time women		Part-time women	
	Best catered for	Worst catered for	Best catered for	Worst catered for
Good pay	21	6	4	9
Security of employment	5	4	5	4
Working conditions	16	3	8	7
Convenient hours	7	1	22	2
Promotion opportunities	4	18	–	6
Worthwhile/interesting work	–	14	–	6
Easy to get to	7	6	1	1
Friendly workmates	17	1	3	–
Understanding supervision	2	14	3	3
Social facilities	2	4	2	–
Trade union branch	–	14	–	4
Shop-steward	–	1	–	2
Work not too difficult	17	3	14	–
No response	11	20	16	34
Total	109	109	78	78

However, we should note that both good pay (12%) and working conditions (9%) were quoted as things worst catered for, together with promotion opportunities and worthwhile work (each 8%). Although these latter two were listed as unimportant, good pay and working conditions were among the most important expectations of this group.

To put these responses in perspective we must appreciate that as many as 44% of this group were unable to find anything that was 'worst catered for'. Altogether it does seem that there was a general level of satisfaction amongst this group, although some 21% felt unable to name anything as best.

Evaluations and importance

So far we have looked at the appraisal of aspects of the job in group terms. In so far as attitudes were similar within each group we can take the predominant answers as indications of the general feelings of the group. In this way we may take aspects which were frequently described as 'best catered for' as those which on the whole the groups felt were well catered for; and similarly those often described as most important may be taken as important to the group. On this basis, a comparison between expectations and perceptions indicates a fair measure of congruence — and so satisfaction — except for the day men.

However, such comparisons must be treated with great caution. Although the evidence from the whole study does indicate a fair degree of homogeneity in the groups we ought not simply to assume it in this case. Accordingly we must also look at the relationship between expectations and perceptions in individual terms. In the first place we will consider the extent to which individuals in each group considered the *most important* aspects of a job were those *best catered for*, as shown in table 4.4.

It is important to realise that describing something as 'best catered for' says nothing about how good the respondent thinks the provision is, except in relation to other aspects. The choice is independent of the overall level of expectations for rewards, which may be expected to vary with commitment

Table 4.4 *Congruence of rating 'best catered for' and 'important' for aspects of the job*

	Proportion rating 'important' aspects 'best catered for'			
Importance attributed to aspect	Day men	Night men	Full-time women	Part-time women
	%	%	%	%
The most important	5	20	8	15
The most *or* second most important	13	24	22	27

to work. Thus, for example, the part-time women may be more easily satisfied in all things but this does not affect their choice of what is best.

Choosing *the* best entailed a forced choice at the extreme where respondents may have had difficulty in distinguishing a single aspect; and the same is true of *the* most important aspect. Thus, bearing in mind the wide spread of answers we would expect very few to choose the same aspect in both cases.

Yet as many as 20% of the night men said the most important aspect was best catered for. This high figure is due almost entirely to satisfaction with security, for two-thirds of those rating security as of first importance in a job also believed this was what their present jobs provided best. The next highest frequency came from the part-time women where 15% thought the most important thing was best catered for. Here, as we would expect, the main item was convenient hours; over a third of those who gave top priority to hours also placed it best in their present job, or looking at it another way, two-thirds of those who thought hours of work was the aspect best catered for regarded them as being of either first or second importance.

Similar congruence between what they felt to be most important and the aspects best provided for was expressed by 8% of full-time women and 5% of day men. These groups were just as likely (9% and 8%) to say most important aspects were worst catered for.

If we take account only of those who gave usable responses to both questions the differences between groups are increased, with congruent responses ranging from 26% on nights to 6% of day men. However, if aspects classed as being of second importance are considered as well, the congruent answers increase faster among the women. The part-time women move into first place with 27% classing the things they regarded as best in their present jobs as among the two most important aspects of any job. They were followed by night men (24%) and full-time women (22%) with the day men far behind (13%). The order is the same if we look at those who felt the best things were the least important; none of the part-time women, 4% of night men, 10% of full-time women and 11% of day men fell in this category. Consideration of proportions rating the two most important things as worst catered for reveals no clear pattern, except that day men were least satisfied with slightly more giving this response than rated these aspects best.

By considering the congruence between the perception of aspects as important and as best catered for, we get a fairly consistent pattern, with the night men and part-time women emerging as the most satisfied groups and the day men as the least satisfied. When we considered the extreme positions of the best provision in the most important aspect, the night men came out on top, but when the range of importance was extended the part-time women were first.

However, these congruent responses represent only a fairly small proportion of each group, covering only the most favourably perceived aspects of the job. Accordingly, respondents were asked to rate all job aspects as 'good', 'average' or 'poor'. This brought in judgements of satisfaction or dissatisfaction for each of the items. As can be seen from table 4.5 the part-time women clearly were most likely to rate their job above average on the aspects they saw as most important. There was little to choose between the full-time women and the night men, while the day men were again the least satisfied. Few rated their most important aspects as below average but, as we would expect, the day men did so most often and the part-time women hardly at all. The responses of the part-time women indicate a particularly high level of satisfaction. However, we must bear in mind that it is probably due, in part, to low expectations following from low involvement in work. To some extent this also applies to the full-time women and explains why

Table 4.5   *Congruence of rating 'good' and 'most important' for aspects of the job*

	Proportion rating 'important' aspects 'good'			
Importance attributed to aspect	Day men	Night men	Full-time women	Part-time women
	%	%	%	%
The most important	43	65	67	82
2nd most important	49	67	62	76

Table 4.6   *Congruence of rating 'good' and 'above average importance' for aspects of the job*

	Proportion rating 'important' aspects 'good'			
Importance attributed to aspect	Day men	Night men	Full-time women	Part-time women
	%	%	%	%
Very important*	41	82	73	88
Important*	63	80	67	82

* The two positions above 'average' on the five-point scale.

they emerge just as satisfied as the night men. Nevertheless our earlier findings (table 4.4) suggest that the high contentment expressed by the women was not simply because their requirements from work were most easily satisfied.

To move away from the extreme position on importance, respondents were asked to rate each item on a five-point scale. This produced a similar pattern of satisfaction on important aspects, as shown in table 4.6. The main points which emerge are that the night shift were closer to the part-time women than to the full-time women, more in line with the pattern of table 4.4, and among the day men less than half of those aspects felt to be very important were rated better than average. This measure has the disadvantage of being vulnerable to different interpretations of 'importance' (as well as 'goodness'), so that those respondents who were more ready to describe aspects as above average importance are overrepresented. Nevertheless, the result does serve to indicate that the pattern of inter-group differences on the more extreme measures with fewer cases also holds at the weaker and more general level.

The judgements of importance also provided a useful basis for looking at the groups' evaluation of specific aspects. As expected, all four groups rated good pay highly as an important feature of the job. Also 63% of the part-time women, 54% of the full-time women and 50% of the night men thought that their pay at Gourmets was better than average. However, only 30% of the day men thought that this applied to their own jobs. Similarly, as we would expect, security of employment was generally considered important, with men stressing it much more than the women. Both groups of men rated this equally highly, while almost all of the night men but only 69% of the day men saw the security of employment at Gourmets as better than average for the area. The full-time women, although less concerned, were just as likely as the day men to think their job security was good (70%), while the part-time women felt less secure than any of the other groups, only 44% of them seeing security at Gourmets as better than average, but they were also the least interested in security. All groups tended to rate working conditions as important and to believe the working conditions at Gourmets to be better than average. Part-time women rated convenient hours much higher than any other group — 72% thought they were important compared with 35% of the full-time women and 16% and 28% of the men on day and night shift respectively. All groups, however, predominantly saw the hours at Gourmets to be better than average for the area. Although a number of men on the night shift looked forward to the four-night week, 74% of them saw the hours to be better than average, while 81% of the day men, 74% of the full-time women and 91% of the part-time women felt the same.

The outstanding features are, again, the high proportion of part-time women who felt hours were both important and well provided for, and of night men giving similar responses with respect to security. The great majority of each of these two groups expressed satisfaction in this way. These responses confirm the trend indicated by the smaller numbers giving the extreme responses of table 4.4.

It seems clear, therefore, that Gourmets tended to meet the basic job expectations of the workforce. With regard to both security and hours of work it seems that the firm more than met the expectations of its employees. A notable exception here again, though, were the men on the day shift who tended to be dissatisfied with both the pay and security aspects of their jobs. In addition to this all groups found the friendliness of their workmates to be well above average, and the job easy to get to from their homes. In each of these the job tended to be over-fulfilling expectations, particularly with the men who, collectively, rated both features with much less importance than the women did. This tendency to over-fulfil expectations is seen in an extreme form when we note that only 22% of the day men, 9% of the night men, 3% of the full-time women and 14% of the part-time women thought good social facilities to be of any real importance in a job, while roughly 60% of each of these groups thought the facilities at Gourmets were better than average.

To this point we have seen that the firm tended to meet or exceed the expectations of the workers and that this was in areas that were mentioned in chapter 3 as the best features of the firm. We would, therefore, expect that if aspects of work failed to meet worker expectation these would be related to the actual work process and the associated controls exercised over him in the job situation. This in fact turned out to be the case. The majority of all groups rated difficulty of job task as of very low importance, while most of them saw their jobs as being easy — in fact too easy. This is substantiated by the fact that, when asked to consider whether or not they were doing worthwhile work, over half of each group thought that their work was less worthwhile than in an average job.

The work process itself was probably the biggest cause of strain for the worker. This had numerous ramifications upon the shop floor behaviour of the worker and influenced his relationship with supervision and the trade union. We will consider these in detail later, but here we should note that the full-time women, as a group, tended to be the only ones to rate the supervisory staff beneath their expectations, while both groups of men tended to focus their criticism upon the promotion system. This latter trend is well defined — 45% of the day men and 30% of the night men rated good promotional prospects as very important while 52% and 83% of these groups saw their prospects at Gourmets to be worse than in an average firm. The women made a similar appraisal of the system, but for them lack of promotion prospects did not appear to be more than slightly important.

DOING THE JOB

Let us look now at the work process itself. We have seen that the production technology had predominantly mass production characteristics which we would expect to be a cause of discontent. The actual content of a job depends on its position in the production process, and not all jobs had these characteristics, particularly those of the day men. Most workers, however, were doing repetitive work on belts, with payment related to output. Table 4.7 reveals an initial analysis of the attitudes of the workers toward the work that they performed.

The first comment we should make is that a high proportion of time workers in each group found their jobs interesting. Time workers were doing a variety of jobs but, compared with piece rate jobs, they tended to have higher levels of responsibility (e.g. inspectors, factory records clerks) or greater freedom of movement and pace (e.g. cleaners and canteen workers). In other words, those who were not subject to pressure from a machine tended to find interest in their work.

The most important point, however, is that 61% of the men on night shift and 50% of the men on day shift found their work basically dull and monotonous with the night men more likely to find no interest at all in their

Table 4.7 *Attitudes to work performance*

	Day men	Night men	Full-time women	Part-time women	All
Interesting all the time	4	4	16	8	32
Interesting most of the time – some dull stretches	28	14	51	47	140
Interesting some of the time – mostly dull and monotonous	25	12	34	13	84
Always dull and monotonous	7	16	8	10	41
Total	64	46	109	78	297

work. In contrast the women were more inclined to find it interesting. In fact 71% of the part-time women found their work basically interesting. These results seem all the more surprising when we remember that the part-time shifts contained a greater proportion of members employed on conveyor-belt operations than any other single group. The point obviously needs more enquiry, and in tables 4.8 and 4.9 we attempt to examine the frustrations and satisfactions that were associated with the work.

Table 4.8   *Are there features of the job that give a sense of achievement?*

	Day men	Night men	Full-time women	Part-time women	All
YES Good product	1	–	1	2	4
YES Doing quota	2	5	18	31	56
YES Intrinsic satisfaction	11	8	12	3	34
Total	14	13	31	36	94
NO Completely boring	24	21	49	25	119
NO Just a job	26	12	29	17	84
Total	50	33	78	42	203

Table 4.8 reveals that 78% of the day men, 72% of the night men, 72% of the full-time women but only 54% of the part-time women saw their work as giving no sense of achievement. However, we should note that of the women who found some satisfaction in their work 58% of the full-time women and 86% of the part-time women found this satisfaction in completing the quota for the shift. The interviewer became convinced during these interviews that this satisfaction was mainly unconnected with the higher wage that such a performance entailed. The women said that they 'felt good' when they knew that they had done what they set out to do, and when they could inform their friends of this fact.[3]

3 Cf. D. Roy, 'Work Satisfaction and Social Reward in Quota Achievement' for an analysis of similar satisfaction among male piece workers.

Table 4.9   *Are there features of the job that give a feeling of frustration?*

	Day men	Night men	Full-time women	Part-time women	All
YES Type of work	19	19	40	15	93
YES Pace of work	1	–	4	6	11
YES Social break down	13	3	16	8	40
YES Mechanical break down	21	8	26	29	84
Total	54	30	86	58	228
NO Repression	8	10	14	17	49
NO Intrinsic satisfaction	2	6	9	3	20
Total	10	16	23	20	69

The importance of this response is increased when we inspect table 4.9. This table shows that 84% of the men on days, 65% of the night shift, 79% of the full-time women and 74% of the part-time women indicated that there were features of the job that made them feel frustrated and irritable. Of those who found nothing that got them down, the overwhelming response was of the form 'If you let it get at you it will drive you mad – I just think of the mortgage and forget about it.' Or as one of the packers on the night shift put it:

> 'It's the kind of job that you can do and not think about. Money's the most important thing here. I wouldn't be in this job if I didn't need the money would I? I'll work hard and get as much in as I can. I offer my body and they pay me for it. I want nothing more to do with them than that.'

These types of responses help to explain why the men on the night shift were less likely to feel frustrated although the most critical of the lack of interest in their jobs. Many of these men mentioned how they 'turned off' when they were on the belts.

While this attempt to cope with the job through 'forgetting about it' was the most common reason given for feeling that there was no source of irritation in the work, a number of workers in each of the groups found their

work to be intrinsically satisfying. Here again we find that the time
workers were atypical; of the twenty responses of this type fifteen came
from workers in this category. This is most clearly demonstrated in the group
of full-time women where eight of the nine responses came from either
factory records clerks or inspectors. One such inspector who was married and
had been with the firm for six years pointed out that,

> 'There is a feeling of achievement when you *know* that you've done a
> good job. For example when you make a decision that you feel is the
> right decision and you have a battle with Production over it. You stick
> by that decision because you know that you've done the right thing.
> That *does* make you feel as if you've done something. It's one of the
> few jobs in this place that you could say that about.'

By far the largest proportion of the workers, however, felt that there were
features of their work which led to feelings of frustration, and although a
special category has been given to those who specified the 'type of work' as
the source of tension, few interviews passed without the words 'monotonous'
and 'boring' being used on some occasion. The time workers again were
less likely to respond in this way but apart from these it would seem that the
nature of work at Brompton had a similar affect upon each of our groups of
workers.

Of all the responses which indicated that there were aspects of the job
which induced tension, the type most often given simply made reference to
the nature of the work itself — 35% of those on days, 63% of the night's,
47% of the full-time women's and 26% of the part-time women's were of this
type. Although all these responses were essentially the same, there were
differences in the way workers in each of the groups tended to articulate
their frustrations. The part-time women, for example, invariably pointed to
the fact that they had 'only to stick it for four hours each day' and 'a morning
isn't too bad, it soon passes'. Frequently they wondered how the women who
worked full-time were able to stick it. The full-time women, particularly the
younger ones, were most likely to make detailed reference to the tensions of
work, as they experienced them. The following examples from some of the
single girls illustrate the way they felt.

A packer aged 19,

> 'When you think about it you can see that there is no point to it at all.
> You've just got to accept it. You'd go mad otherwise.'

A packer aged 18,

> 'I go terrible sometimes just thinking about coming to work in the
> mornings. It's not hard work but it seems to wear you out. When you
> don't talk it's terrible — it's a real drag — you could scream. Someone
> went like that last week. You've just got to control yourself.'

A service girl, aged 17,

'My nerves have been terrible since I came here. I've lost three stone altogether. I needed to I suppose but it's gone beyond a joke now. I'm getting really jumpy, and very irritable too. Especially when I'm at home, especially with my little brother. It gets everyone though. A girl on one of the belts near me went screaming around the department last week. It's doing the same thing day after day that does it.'

A weigher, aged 24,

'You can't imagine how boring it is. It can really get you down. The girls are O.K. – they're great. It's just the job. The job is terrible.'

Although none of the men spoke of 'screaming', their references to the type of work were essentially the same – it was tedious and monotonous. Where they differed was in the extent to which the men understood the nature of the work in the wider context of their lives, as they were and as they might be. Frequently the men on the day shift compared their job with other more 'ideal' jobs and expressed discontent that they did not have, *and never would have* such a job. Two responses make this point clearer:

A trucker aged 25, married with one child,

'Now if it was taking an engine apart or something, that would really interest me. You'd be *doing* something then. You're not doing anything in this job. You just try to get by with a laugh and a joke.'

A service boy aged 17,

'I'm browned off practically every day. You're just doing the same thing every day. It would be different if you were making something. It's just the same old thing. There's no chance to get on, either. It's just the same old thing, all around you, stretching out for ever. That's what get's me most I think – that it will go on for ever.'

These responses were similar to those given by some full-time women who were single and had been in the factory for a number of years. One 32-year-old, single women who was an operator of a wrapping machine, pointed out that,

'It's worse just before and after the holidays. It's not a worthwhile job and the holidays bring it home to you. The monotony can get you very depressed – you're inclined to take the job home with you. You've nothing to think about in these sort of jobs and you end up thinking about yourself.'

There is a slight difference between these sorts of response and the responses given by the men on nights. For, while men on the day shift did mention the money, as did the married women who worked full-time on the belts, the night men were most likely to couch their discontent in terms of economic coercion. As one man put it,

'The jobs here are deadly. It's the worst job I've had as far as boredom goes. It really gets me down sometimes – the thought that to get the money you've got to keep going on and on all the time at the same thing.'

It is, perhaps, a little surprising that so few workers mentioned the pace of work as a source of tension. All but one who did mention it were women and all were belt auxiliaries or, in the case of some of the part-time women, had no permanent job but usually worked as auxiliaries. Thus complaints about pace came not from those working directly on the belts but those who serviced them. In spite of the small numbers involved, this flies in the face of our original assumptions about the nature of this type of work, and the evidence presented by other studies of mass production systems. We had expected that the nature of the auxiliaries' task would make it more likely for these workers to be able to 'make their own time'. However, when we examine these responses, we find that all of them take the form of this statement made by a young girl who serviced some of the belts in Big Block.

'The worst thing is when the girls on the belts start shouting for something and you can't get it. When you've been working hard, and there's tins on the floor that the girls have thrown down, and its very hot, and you just *can't* get the things that they want. It's not your fault, you can't help it, you've been working hard but the things are just not there.'

On short belts, where the 'components' are small and the pace fast, the nature of 'auxiliary' work can be very different from the work of 'sub-assemblers' in car factories. The rate of turnover in 'components' is much more rapid and the restrictions on storage near the belts means that the auxiliaries are unlikely to be able to build up very large 'banks' of 'components' and so are dominated by the production process. Their intermediary position between the manufacturing and packing processes means, moreover, that they are likely to be caught in the cross fire of any conflict.

Although these responses did relate to the actual pace of the work done by auxiliaries, they made implicit reference to the structure of workshop relationships and had a great deal in common with the responses that specifically mentioned 'social' or 'mechanical' breakdowns as the chief source of tension. Mechanical breakdowns were mentioned continually; half of the part-time women who found their work to be frustrating at times indicated this as the source, while about 30% of the other groups did likewise. These breakdowns had the obvious initial annoyance of preventing the workers reaching their quota targets, and this we remember was highly quoted in table 4.8 as giving a sense of achievement. In addition to this, such breakdowns interrupt the work routine. They make the worker think more about the actual work process, so repression through conversation becomes more difficult, and above all they make the worker feel powerless to affect the situation. Frequently women mentioned that the worst thing was to be sitting at the belt not knowing when it would start again. Furthermore, the 'social breakdowns' mentioned by the women were nearly always related to these mechanical breakdowns. Conflicts with supervision and the maintenance staff, together with irritability within the work group, are likely to be a concomitant of mechanical failure.

It is interesting again to compare these attitudes to those of workers on automobile production tracks who valued breakdowns as an escape from the monotony. One worker interviewed by Chinoy, for example, said that, 'You get the feeling, everyone gets the feeling, whenever the line jerks, everyone is wishing "breakdown, baby"'.[4] When the track does break down few of the automobile workers come into direct contact with the repair operations; for most of them the breakdown in the line is also a breakdown in control, they are able to smoke, play cards or 'fool around'. Not so at Gourmets, however. Firstly the packing belts are much shorter and more tightly spaced than the automobile track – there is no room to play cards let alone fool around. Secondly the rules in the factory prevent workers from smoking or moving away from their work station. So a mechanical breakdown at Gourmets leaves the workers standing around their conveyor belt while the repairs are made. Now, while the belt controls the worker it does mean that during normal operations belt workers are effectively free from supervisory control. During breakdowns, however, the workers come under the direction of the supervisors, and this, together with the inconvenience and loss of wages, makes the stoppage anything but a breakdown of control. Instead of a relaxing interlude it becomes a period of frustration charged with latent conflicts.

A final point here is that eight of the thirteen day men who mentioned 'social breakdown' were time workers. These, we have pointed out, were mostly older men who had previously held higher status jobs – one or two had been supervisors. Typical responses here came from cleaners whose annoyance stemmed from their perception of their own status as lower than that of their work contacts. Objections to the production men 'idling around and getting paid good money for it', or to them walking over newly cleaned

4 E. Chinoy, *Automobile Workers and the American Dream*, p. 17. See also
   C. R. Walker and R. H. Guest, *The Man on the Assembly Line* and
   R. Blauner, *Alienation and Freedom*.

floors, were often made. These workers were generally conscious of their low status in the firm, and consequently they tended to be most critical of those aspects of the organisation entailing social relationships which brought out this lack of status. For instance, their attitudes toward supervision and the union tended to parallel the responses that we have noted in connection with their jobs.

Desire for a change
Respondents were asked next whether, if they were given freedom to do so, they would like to change their job for any other in the factory. The results are shown in table 4.10.

Table 4.10   *Preference for a change of job*

	Day men	Night men	Full-time women	Part-time women	All
YES More interesting	20	˙19	38	13	90
YES Other	17	4	4	7	32
Total	37	23	42	20	122
NO All monotonous	12	9	13	13	47
NO Miss work group	2	2	34	21	59
NO Satisfied	13	12	20	24	69
Total	27	23	67	58	175

The men of both shifts were more inclined to favour change in their jobs than the women; 58% of the day men and 50% of the night men, compared with 39% of the full-time women and 26% of the part-time women, elected to change their jobs if given the opportunity. The desire for a more interesting job was common to all groups, though less important among the part-time women where only 17% felt this strongly enough to want a different job, in contrast to 41% of the men on nights. Altogether, three-quarters of those who wanted a change did so because they felt their present jobs were not sufficiently interesting, and only among the day men did a substantial number give any other reason. Desire for promotion, better working conditions, more pay and a chance to see other parts of the factory are grouped under 'other', together with one female aspirant who professed a marked inclination toward the job of personnel manager.

In view of the answers on job satisfaction the numbers not wishing to change jobs may seem surprising. The most quoted reason for immobility among the women was removal from the work group — 51% of full-time women and 36% of part-time women not wishing to change offered this as their reason. This, too was the main reason for women wishing to stay at Gourmets (table 3.9). It appears, therefore, that the work group played a dominant part in providing the female worker with satisfaction in her work at Gourmets.

FRIENDSHIPS AT WORK

The dominance of this trend is substantiated by the information in tables 4.11 and 4.12, with regard to the full-time women, but the part-time women's responses appear rather surprising at first sight. The full-time women were more inclined than any other group to be on close friendly terms with other members of the work group, and to have a particular friend in the department. It is clear, however, that the men on night shift

Table 4.11 *Degree of friendliness with members of the work group*

	Day men	Night men	Full-time women	Part-time women	All
Extremely	34	23	60	34	151
Quite friendly	29	23	49	44	145
Indifferent	1	—	—	—	1
Total	64	46	109	78	297

Table 4.12 *Incidence of a 'particular friend' in the worker's department*

	Day men	Night men	Full-time women	Part-time women	All
A friend	32	14	70	36	152
No friend	32	32	39	42	145
Total	64	46	109	78	297

and the part-time women were less likely than the other groups to have developed close friendship attachments in the work place.

To explain this we must first take account of opportunity. On the part-time shifts there was a high turnover of personnel and the women tended to have worked at the firm for a shorter time than the other groups. Also, the time they spent at work in any day was shorter. Thus, the part-time women had had less opportunity to make friends, and if they had, their friends were more likely to have left. This goes some way to explaining what might otherwise be a surprising absence of close friendships among the part-time women.

The foregoing argument cannot be applied to the men on nights. However, there is a further limitation on opportunity which does apply to both groups. This is the fact that the part-time women and night-shift men were less likely to have a permanent job than workers in other groups, and those with relatively permanent jobs were still more likely to be moved around between jobs, and so between work groups. That this was continually stressed by the women as a source of complaint is linked with the fact that their nomadic employment position not only prevented them from making an adequate adjustment to a regular work routine but also, and more importantly, it prevented them from developing a stable friendship group in their department.

Another point of considerable importance is that these two groups had higher proportions of workers with families. These workers would be more family centred and so less likely to develop close friendships with their workmates. Throughout the sample, those with children were rather less likely to describe their friendliness with fellow workers as extreme, and much less likely to have a particular friend at work. Consequently friendships were less intense in the groups with more family men and women. Unlike some other night workers,[5] those at Gourmets did not find their unusual hours threw them together outside work because they could not take part in 'ordinary' social life; they turned to their families instead. The part-time women wanted a pleasant friendly atmosphere at work, but once again we find they gave primacy to their family roles.

If we make allowance for these various factors the differences between groups largely disappear, but it still seems that women were rather more likely to be on very friendly terms with their workmates. It is clear that friendships played an important part in the worklives of these people. However, it should be remembered that less than a quarter of them saw friendly relationships as an essential part of their job.

---

5 E.g. the printers studied in S. M. Lipset *et al.*, *Union Democracy*.

The limited importance they gave to work group friendships is illustrated by the splitting up of work groups in the canteen. The majority of the sample took their meals in the canteen, and it is interesting to note that a particular pattern of stable 'eating groups' had developed. While 54% of the day men took their meals with members of their work group, only 35% of the night shift and 23% of the full-time women did so. For these latter groups, meals tended to be taken with people whom they met, either at work or in the canteen, when they first arrived – 63% of the night shift and 54% of the full-time women ate their meals in these types of groups.

PAYMENT SYSTEM

Finally in this chapter we shall examine the payment system. This, together with the work process, is an important component of the control system, as it is by this means that the individual worker can relate his actual effort to his monetary reward – a fundamental part of the 'effort bargain'.[6] The literature on the relative merits of various types of payment procedures is voluminous and in general inconclusive.[7] It cannot be claimed that workers will work harder in all situations under one or other of the various forms of payment systems. What is fairly certain, however, is that most occupational groups[8] will use the formal rules of any payment system as a means of regulating the level of their pay and as a result controlling an important aspect of their lives at work.[9]

A fundamental precondition of this process is that the members of the occupation understand the method of payment and how it applies to them. It is, therefore, highly significant that, when we discount all time workers, over three-quarters of the men, 92% of the full-time women and virtually all of the part-time women had no idea how their pay was calculated. All those who understood had had the system explained to them over a period of time by the supervision, while 48% of the day men, 90% of the night men, 82% of the full-time women and 68% of the part-time women who didn't understand had also had the system explained to them without success. The interviewer heard the phrase 'it would take a Philadelphia lawyer to understand it'

6 H. Behrend, 'The Effort Bargain'. W. Baldamus, *Efficiency and Effort.*
7 For a discussion of this literature see R. Marriott, *Incentive Payment Schemes.*
8 The literature on 'restriction of output' and other patterns of control has tended to concentrate upon manual occupations. E. C. Hughes, 'The Sociological Study of Work' has suggested, however, that such restriction of output characterises white-collar occupations equally.
9 For a brilliantly insightful description of such a process see D. Roy, 'Efficiency and "The Fix" '.

applied to the payment system several times in every day. The incomprehensibility of the pay cards had entered the folk lore of the factory. It is little wonder that several regarded this as the worst thing about the firm. This response by a man on the day shift was typical:

'The pay card — it's got all those queer numbers on it and columns with "what Gourmets give you" and "what you've earned". It's bloody crazy. One of the lads said to me to take no notice of the other side. I'm baffled by it. I usually compare mine with my mate's — he's baffled as well.'

The system was a new one, which might go some way to explain the difficulty. However, the situation became more complicated when respondents were asked if they preferred the new pay system to the old. Well over half of the part-time women were not aware that the system had been changed, while 28% of the full-time women and 14% of the men were placed in a similar state of amazement by the question. Of those who were aware of a new system, large numbers didn't know how they felt about it, while among those who had formulated some positive opinion, feelings were clearly mixed, with a majority of all but the night shift expressing views that were in one way or another antagonistic to the new system. The apparent incomprehensibility of the payment system was a source of tension which we might have expected to become focused in direct criticism of the pay received, but in fact permeated other aspects of work. Doubtless it led to some dissatisfaction about pay. In general, however, the workers' concern was not so much with the level of pay, which compared favourably with wages elsewhere in the area, but its method of calculation. Consequently the strain related to the control system rather than the economic rewards.

Lack of understanding made it impossible for the workforce to relate their actions as producers to their pay and so exercise some control over their payment. The workers were forced to resort to a rule of thumb method of comparison with the wages of others, and any discrepancy, which might well be a perfectly legitimate one in the eyes of management and also the shop-stewards, was seized upon, because the formal and informal appraisal of wages were completely different. Management might be 'putting one over' on them, and no amount of explanation by a supervisor or shop-steward could be sufficient to remove the workers' suspicions because it was not understood — effectively they were talking different languages. The conflict which is latent in such a situation is likely to manifest itself during periods of strain. Thus mechanical breakdown tended to bring conflicts into the open, because in this situation the worker was annoyed anyway and was likely to fasten this annoyance on to the tangibility of 'how will our pay be affected?' This, of course, could not be explained in a way which was comprehensible, and conflict was increased. In fact a situation of just this type resulted in a series of strikes by women belt workers in one department shortly after the introduction of the new payment system. More generally this throws light on the antagonism engendered by mechanical breakdown and the concern about all aspects of the control system.

SUMMARY

Good pay and security of employment were seen by the men to be of basic importance in a job. Working conditions and opportunities for promotion were of additional importance, especially to the day men, while some of the night shift also attached importance to convenient hours. Although not regarded as of prime importance, there was also a feeling that work should be worthwhile and interesting.

The women regarded pay as important but gave rather more weight to good working conditions, while the part-time women gave top priority to convenient working hours. Security was accorded some importance, mainly by the full-time women, but did not generally have the basic significance that it had for the men, while promotion opportunities were regarded as of little consequence. However, friendly relationships with the people at work, which seemed to matter little to the men, were fairly important to the women. Clearly the different orientations of the women, as indicated by their priorities, reflect their roles in the wider society. Many of those who were not already married were young and likely to be married later, while those who remained single were less likely than the men to have dependants to support. Thus, less committed to work by economic necessity, with no interest in 'getting on', they wanted to work with pleasant people in good conditions, while those already married also wanted to work hours which would fit in with their family responsibilities.

In general the firm fulfilled the basic job expectations of the workers. The part-time women and men on night shift were the most contented groups because the firm was seen to be satisfying their basic demands of convenient hours and security of employment. Indeed, to a high degree the part-time women felt that in their present jobs their most important expectations were well catered for. The full-time women also tended to be quite satisfied in this sense, in some ways just as much as the night men, though there was less consensus in evaluating job aspects. The men on day shift were the least contented, being less enthusiastic about both the level of pay and the security of employment than other groups.

In spite of this general satisfaction, however, certain aspects of the jobs at Gourmets tended to be criticised. The firm had more social facilities, and was more conveniently located than most workers expected, but the structure of promotional opportunities for the men, especially the day men, and the relationship between the supervisors and the full-time women tended to be areas of conflict.

Discontent, however, tended to be focused around the type and organisation of work at the factory. There was little intrinsic job satisfaction; on the contrary the work was generally felt to be frustrating, uninteresting and giving no sense of achievement. Over three-quarters of the respondents found their work was apt to be frustrating, with the day men complaining most and the night men least. Most found their work was uninteresting at times and almost half felt it was basically uninteresting. The night men were less satisfied than those on days, as might be expected from the difference in their types of work, since the night-shift jobs were mainly machine-controlled mass production. On the same basis we would expect the women to be no more satisfied than the night men but this was not so; the women were much more likely than the men to feel that their work was interesting. The part-time women were also more likely to derive some sense of achievement from their work, but even in this group a majority gained no such satisfaction. Altogether, there was considerable dissatisfaction in this area. This was heightened by a seemingly incomprehensible payment system, especially at times of strain such as when the belts broke down.

The tendency for the women to be less discontented with their work appears to be due to lower expectations, and also to the conversations that they had with their workmates and the songs they sang with Radio Caroline on the Tanhoy. In keeping with this, the women were less keen to change to more interesting jobs in the firm, mainly because they were unwilling to leave their friends. The part-time women, with generally lower commitment to work, were most satisfied with their present jobs and not bothered about lack of interest, while among those who didn't want to change, reluctance to leave workmates was more important for the full-time women. However, the part-time women were less likely to be in stable work groups anyway, which was a cause of dissatisfaction to them. It was also one of the factors leading to less close friendships amongst them, the other causes being less time spent at work and, like the night men, greater family-centredness.

Before leaving this chapter, a word about the analysis of job satisfaction may be useful. The usual approach, in studies which have gone beyond a direct simple question, has been to score respondents' dissatisfaction/ satisfaction on particular aspects, then on the basis of this to evaluate the contribution of the aspects. However, in keeping with the general approach of this study, this is regarded as inadequate since it takes no account of what people expect from work. Different people have different wants and expectations, and satisfaction with the total job depends on how adequately they feel the most salient of these are met. Accordingly, we have not only looked at satisfaction with various aspects of the job, but have related this to evaluations of relative importance and taken the congruence between estimates of importance and perceptions of good provision as an indication of job satisfaction or commitment to their jobs.

The consequence of such an approach is well illustrated by our findings for the night shift. The type of work involved in their jobs was such as might lead to a prediction of frustration and discontent.[10] Indeed they were dissatisfied with this aspect of their work — they complained more than any other group about uninteresting work and were the most eager to change to more interesting jobs. However, most of them attached relatively low importance to having intrinsically satisfying or worthwhile work, while they were, on the whole, satisfied with the aspects they felt were important. Consequently they were pretty well satisfied with their jobs, and although many would gladly change to something more interesting it would have to be something which did not alter the salient rewards of their present employment situation.

To understand the different patterns of job satisfaction which we have observed in the Brompton workforce, we must also take account of involvement in work, as distinct from involvement in the firm or job.[11] While job satisfaction depends on the relation between the levels of rewards and the relative importance of different job aspects, it will also be affected by the overall importance of work for the individual. Involvement in work varies according to the way work is related to other aspects of a person's life. Here there appear to be two crucial factors which are clearly interrelated, namely the degree of economic necessity and the extent to which a person's identity is defined, socially and by the individual, through work or other roles. At Gourmets commitment to work was lowest among the part-time women, who gave primacy to their position within the family, and highest among the men with dependants to support.

On the whole the experience of work at Gourmets was not particularly rewarding.[12] The part-time women have emerged as quite well satisfied, but this is largely a consequence of the low importance they attached to work, and their satisfaction stemmed more from the convenience of the job for family life than from their experience of work. The full-time women enjoyed the friendly company of their workmates — an aspect of the situation they

---

10 See, for example, R. Blauner, *Alienation and Freedom.*
11 See Etzioni, *A Comparative Analysis of Complex Organisations*, for a discussion of involvement.
12 The few exceptions were mainly among the non-manual time workers.

created for themselves, but in spite of this and their relatively low commitment to work they were only moderately satisfied. The day men had high expectations and were the most dissatisfied. The only group with high work involvement and fairly high satisfaction were the night men, but this does not mean that they liked their jobs. The satisfaction of the night men rested on the belief that 'men must work' and that their position in the labour market was such that all jobs open to them which paid a 'reasonable' wage were broadly the same — they were all boring. Given this and the fact that their family position prevented them from going to sea or becoming lorry drivers, the basic requirement in a job was security, and this at least was good at Gourmets. Commitment was not so much to the job as the firm providing the job. Such commitment has little affective content, being primarily an evaluation of the firm as a better than average provider of the basic requirements of their (unfortunate) need to work.

5 The worker and supervision

In this chapter and the one that follows, we intend to develop the findings of the preceding chapters, by relating them to two specific aspects of the work environment: supervision, and the consultative and negotiation machinery. These are two vital aspects of the control system. We would expect the differences which we have already noted between the groups of workers to result in different perceptions of, and attitudes toward these two institutions.

WORKERS' VIEWS ABOUT BEING A SUPERVISOR

For the worker, the supervisor represents at one and the same time the lowest level of managerial control and the main opening for upward mobility within the factory. We would expect that the extent to which a worker aspired to a supervisory role would be related to the perception of supervision which he gained in the work place, and the degree to which work was centrally important in his life. Desire for promotion may be taken as an indicator of involvement in the firm,[1] but on a rather different plane from the positive involvement we have observed among the instrumentally orientated night men. The nature of the supervisory job, the greater responsibilities associated with it, and its structural location outside the work group are likely to lead to aspirants for such positions possessing some 'moral' commitment to the organisation.

We found that only two of the day men, eight of the night men, five of the full-time women and three of the part-time women had previously applied for a supervisory position. Of these, the two day men, three of the night men and one part-time woman were still interested in becoming supervisors, although all of them felt dissatisfied with the method of selection. Similar dissatisfaction was quoted as the reason for loss of interest by the other ex-applicants.

Table 5.1 indicates the reasons given by the rest of the sample for their non-application. When the respondents were asked to explain why they hadn't applied to be supervisors, about half the men and over 80% of the women gave answers indicating that they didn't want the job. A large proportion of each group simply remarked that they had 'no interest' in promotion.

---

1 See J. A. Banks, *Industrial Participation.*

Table 5.1   *Reasons for non-application for promotion to supervisor*

	Day men	Night men	Full-time women	Part-time women	All
No interest	18	15	43	12	88
Lose friends	2	1	19	11	33
Too much responsibility	10	2	12	13	37
No ability	2	–	11	7	20
Not here long enough	15	8	14	17	54
Wouldn't get the job	14	9	2	3	28
'Part-time'[2]	–	–	–	12	12
Other	1	3	3	–	7
All non-applicants	62	38	104	75	279

Among the remainder there was a marked difference between men and women. The women were much more likely to give reasons relating to aspects of the supervisory job. Many were unwilling to take on the responsibility attached to the role, they felt that they hadn't the ability to carry it out, or they feared the loss of friends which might accompany its performance. Several men also didn't want the responsibility but they were less likely to worry about their ability or loss of friends. Over 40% of the women gave these reasons related to the supervisory role, compared with 23% of the day men and only 7% of the night shift. On the other hand both groups of men (23% of the day men and 24% of the night men) were inclined to explain their non-application for the job by reference to the selection procedure. The interviewer frequently heard reference to nepotism, 'having a face that fits', and also, oddly enough, membership of the firm's bowling club and the badge that goes with it, as features of the selection procedure.

One of the criteria felt to be important for selection of supervisory personnel was length of service. All groups frequently mentioned this as a reason for non-application. Since this type of response was, of course, limited to workers with relatively short lengths of service, the dominance of this type of answer is quite striking. It seems certain that the figures underestimate the importance of this factor from the employees' viewpoint, and that a belief in

---

2   This response came from those who thought there were no part-time supervisors, so that they had no chance. In fact there were a few part-time supervisors, but the estimate of promotion prospects was about right.

selection on the basis of length of service was common among the longer service personnel as well.

Most workers consider length of service, and with it the essential knowledge of the jobs in the factory, to be a basic prerequisite for a promotional aspirant. Length of service is also important for its use in the attempt by workers to exercise some control over their market situation. As we have previously pointed out, most occupational groups attempt to obtain such control. Chinoy,[3] for example, has shown how workers in automobile factories operated a 'long-service' rule to control access to valued subassembly operations. So the 'long-service' rule can be seen to reflect both the status hierarchy within the workgroup and also the rational attempt by workers to protect their interests within the employment situation. Length of service, therefore, plays an important part in the workers' informal assessment of the supervisory selection procedure. All other things being equal, the long-serving worker should be preferred to one of short service — seniority usually being seen by workers as the only objectively observable criterion for promotion which is legitimate. Management, however, will often prefer other, less tangible criteria in order to select supervisors whom they judge to be of the 'right type'. Consequently the actual criteria used are liable to be ill understood and to conflict with the interests and evaluations of the workers. As in the case of the payment system, this resulted in a situation structured by lines of latent conflict. Hence the general current of dissatisfaction with promotion procedures which we have noted on several occasions, and a strong tendency for explanations of selection to be in terms of nepotism and other related phenomena. We shall see the importance of this as the argument develops.

Advantages

Table 5.2 reveals what the workers considered were the best things to be gained from being a supervisor. It should be noted that in this and other such tables in this chapter, few people gave more than one response. This indicates that, in contrast to the examination of the firm in chapter 3, where respondents frequently gave two responses, we are now probing what are for many workers the fringes of their work experience.

Thirteen of the full-time women were unable to answer this question, while a further thirty of them, together with nine part-time women and twelve of the men, could think of nothing attractive about the role of supervisor. All in all, a quarter of the respondents were unable to give a positive response of any sort to this question, the proportion ranging from

---

3 E. Chinoy, *Automobile Workers and The American Dream.*

Table 5.2 *Best thing about being a supervisor**

Response	Day men No.	%	Night men No.	%	Full-time women No.	%	Part-time women No.	%
Pay	9	14	10	22	8	7	26	33
Status	22	34	5	11	7	6	18	23
Fringe benefits	4	6	9	20	13	12	6	8
Security	8	13	6	13	–	–	–	–
Intrinsic satisfaction	16	25	16	35	25	23	18	23
Help people	1	2	2	4	5	5	–	–
Easy job	8	13	3	7	16	15	6	8
Ego satisfaction	6	9	1	2	10	9	2	3
Nothing	7	11	5	11	30	28	9	12
Don't know	1	2	2	4	13	12	6	8
Total responses	82	128	59	128	127	116	91	117

* As in other tables of this type, two responses were allowed so the number of responses lies between 100% and 200%. See note to table 3.2.

13% of day men (the group most interested in promotion) to 39% of full-time women. In all departments the full-time women gave a consistently high number of 'nothing' or 'don't know' responses, which seems to indicate that this group found itself more isolated from or antagonistic toward the supervisory personnel than the other groups.

Before we examine the table in detail we should recognise that the respondents used two different approaches in assessing the supervisor's job. They were asked what they considered to be the most attractive thing offered to people who held the position of supervisor. Most of the responses to this question indicated that the respondents could see advantages to be gained from being a supervisor which they themselves would want. On the other hand a minority of the workers were out of sympathy with the main satisfactions which they considered supervisors derived from the job. The distinction is most apparent between the responses 'status' and 'ego satisfaction'. The former were based upon an evaluation of the supervisory role within the hierarchy of the organisation. They indicated, to some extent, acceptance of the supervisory role as one of legitimate authority, and also one toward which the respondent might aspire. A typical response here was of the form: 'You'd feel as if you'd got somewhere. You would have bettered yourself then, wouldn't you?' On the other hand, the 'ego satisfaction' group tended to appraise the supervisor rather than the role: 'They think that they're that bit better than you'. 'They won't talk to you any more'. 'They just want that armband'. These responses, therefore, together with those which claimed that supervisors had an easy job, were essentially critical of supervision. To these we may tentatively add the number of respondents who saw nothing that could be attractive in the supervisory position. It is interesting to note that the full-time women and the day men were more likely to give answers of this type.

In assessing the supervisory position, we can distinguish at the analytical level between the socio-economic benefits which accompany the role, and the actual behaviour entailed in the performance of the role. It is of interest to note that all but the full-time women stressed the former aspects in their assessment of 'the best thing'. However, the emphasis varied between the groups. Only the men mentioned the supervisors' greater security, while pay was stressed most by the part-time women. The night men, as we would expect, saw economic rewards as important but their responses were spread between pay, fringe benefits and security. The status of the role was the feature referred to most often by the day men and also frequently by the part-time women, but received few mentions from the other groups. The high rating given to this by the day men is perhaps predictable, in the light of this group's professed discontent with their present jobs and their desire for better ones. For the part-time women the explanation is rather different. We have already noted that they were different in their attitudes and reasons for work. On the whole they were older and more likely to have children than their full-time counterparts; many were driven to work by economic need, and others in a conscious search for friendship. Furthermore they spent only half the time that other groups spent in the factory. Consequently their involvement in the factory was much lower than any other group, and more easily justified in terms of money, convenience, and friendship than anything else. Under these circumstances it appears that the part-time women were much more prepared than any other group to accept the factory for what it is. This low involvement often led them to appraise aspects of the work situation from a perspective 'one removed' from the situation itself. Thus their detached view of supervisors led to the sort of assessment illustrated in this typical response referring to the status of the supervisor's role: 'I don't know much about it really, but I should imagine that they feel as if they'd done something, or made something of themselves'. The emphasis of this type of response contrasts with those given by the full-time workers.

When we look at the responses relating to features of the supervisory work itself, the effects of dissatisfactions become clearer. Responses of this nature tend to draw upon the respondents' actual work experience in connection with supervision, as a basis of appraisal. All four groups gave eminence to the intrinsic satisfaction that can be gained from the freedom associated with the supervisory role – this would seem to be related to the lack of intrinsic satisfaction which these respondents found in their own work. However, as we saw, the full-time women and the day men were more inclined than other groups to give responses that were antagonistic toward the supervisory function. Fifteen per cent of the full-time women and 13% of the day men thought that it was 'just an easy job', while 9% of these groups saw the role as a mechanism for satisfying the ego of its incumbent.

Disadvantages

Turning to the worst thing about the supervisory role, in table 5.3, again we have a high percentage of respondents who could see nothing bad about being a supervisor or who didn't know what the worst thing could be. The pattern of responses within each group is remarkably similar throughout this table. The main cleavage is between the night shift and all other groups. Only 7% of this group thought that the loss of friends would be the worst thing, while over a quarter of the other groups gave this response. All groups gave equal stress to the responsibility of the role, and the marginality that is associated with it, while a substantial number thought that control of the workers would

Table 5.3   *Worst thing about supervisory role*

	Day men		Night men		Full-time women		Part-time women	
	No.	%	No.	%	No.	%	No.	%
Lose friends	17	27	3	7	34	31	22	28
Control of workers	9	14	13	28	22	20	18	23
Responsibility	18	28	13	28	22	20	25	32
Marginality	8	13	6	13	9	8	10	13
Other	1	2	–	–	2	2	–	–
Nothing	14	22	12	26	21	19	12	15
Don't know	2	3	3	7	8	7	4	5
Total responses	69	108	50	109	118	108	91	117

be the most difficult feature of the role. It is interesting to note that the more children the women had, the less likely were they to worry about controlling workers. Somewhat surprisingly, however, there was no tendency for older women (or older men) to worry less on this score.

In their appraisal of the worst features of the supervisory role all groups concentrated upon the actual work task of the supervisor, and the relationship that this produced between him (or her) and the workers. There seemed a general acceptance of the socio-economic advantages which the role offers, but these were (as we shall see later) considered legitimate primarily because of the drawbacks that are associated with being a supervisor. The difference between the responses of the night shift and the other groups is worthy of further comment at this point, to see why this shift quoted loss of friends much less often than any other group. The night men, we saw, tended to be less attached to their job at Gourmets through friendships than the other groups, and also were less likely to take advantage of opportunities to establish close friendships. This is one variable of explanation, another being that the supervision on night shift was different from that on the day shift. In other words, occupying a supervisory role on the night shift was not accompanied by the loss of friendship links with the work group. Both variables are, in fact, of importance. The night men were less inclined to be concerned with friendship ties, while the supervision on the shift tended to be less formal than on the day shift. This informality may well be related to the fact that proportionately twice as many responses indicating difficulty in controlling the workers were received from the night men as from the day men. This, however, is a complex phenomenon which is related to the level of unionisation on the shift, so we will consider it at greater length in the next chapter.

THE SUPERVISORS

The information contained in table 5.4 conforms with what we would have expected on the basis of the analysis so far. Over three-quarters of the part-time women maintained that the right people were selected while two-thirds of the day men said that on average the wrong people occupied supervisory positions. The night men and the full-time women marginally elected that the right people were not promoted. It will be recalled that the full-time women and day men were most critical of supervision, while the men were more concerned about promotion.

Among the women expressing approval of the selection procedure, the most usual explanation, especially in Big Block, was that the supervisory staff were considerate in their treatment of the workers. Almost half of each group

Table 5.4 *In general are the right people chosen as supervisors?*

	Day men	Night men	Full-time women	Part-time women	All
Yes	18	22	52	62	154
No	43	24	57	16	140
Don't know	3	–	–	–	3
Total	64	46	109	78	297

mentioned this as substance to their claim. In addition about a third of both groups made comments to the effect that the supervisory staff were of 'the right calibre'. Often this response hinged upon the supervisors' treatment of the workers. The 'right calibre' for female supervisors was seen as 'the job not going to their heads', 'you can approach them about anything', and so on. This trend was borne out in the reasons of those who thought the wrong people were chosen. Eighty-two per cent of the full-time women and 75% of the part-time women who were critical of the selection procedure maintained that the supervisory staff were unsympathetic in their relationships with the workers. All these responses tended to develop similar themes – 'favouritism', 'two-facedness' and an inability to 'handle the girls' were continually mentioned. A few examples may help to demonstrate this:

'There's a lot of favouritism in this block. Supervisors should be nice to *all* the girls and give them *all* a fair chance. They should try to make the girls feel wanted. When you come here first and you haven't got a permanent job you feel just as if you're going to market. As if you're just standing around waiting to be sold.'

'They're all inclined to be two-faced. They won't fight for you, yet they're scared to death of you at the same time. They won't come back to you and tell you what has happened.'

'They've got some real shockers here. Their attitude to the girls seems to be "you're just a worker". They really look down their noses at you.'

'Some of them are really stern. They don't seem to know the first thing about how to get girls to do things. They should look after the girls – see that they've settled down; take an interest in you. The girls would appreciate that.'

For the woman worker, therefore, an essential prerequisite for a good supervisor was that she be 'human relations orientated'. Many of the full-time women felt that their supervisor should 'stick up for the girls on the belt'. A good supervisor was one who looked after 'her girls'.

The part-time women's much greater propensity to believe that the right people were selected, which is revealed in table 5.4, becomes even more outstanding when we realise that both groups of women tended to utilise the same yardstick for the appraisal of supervisory ability. Substance is given to the thesis that the part-time women are more inclined to accept the factory situation as it is, by the fact that 21% of the responses in favour of supervision were based upon the belief that 'Gourmets know what they are doing – they wouldn't pick anyone unless they knew that she'd be able to do the job'. However, this alone cannot explain the difference between the groups. It appears that although both groups of women tended to appraise supervisory ability on the same basis, the norm of 'being nice to people' differed from group to group. Because of her higher involvement and longer time at work, the full-time woman expected more of her supervisor in terms of 'looking after the girls' than did the part-time woman. This discrepancy between the norms of each group was accentuated by the fact that the part-time woman, because of her age, was treated with greater respect anyway. In other words the part-time women were more likely to think that the supervisors were nice to them partly because they were more easily satisfied, but also because to a great extent the supervisors actually were nicer to them.

Both groups of men also referred to supervisory inability to 'treat people properly'. Among the men who claimed that the wrong people were promoted, 42% of each group quoted this. However, the men were much more likely to base their criticism upon the job ability of the supervisory staff than were the women. Two-thirds of the night men and 40% of the day men, but only 23% of the women, who criticised their supervision did so on the grounds that they didn't know their job. Also, over 20% of these groups claimed that the selection procedure was immoral, compared with 7% of the women. It is interesting to note that many of the responses which quoted this criticism were given in addition to another response. The belief in the immorality of the selection procedure was continually backed with evidence which drew attention to the discrepancy between the worker's values and expectations and the formal operation of the promotional system. We noted earlier that length of service was an informally agreed criterion for supervisory selection among the workforce, and the stress laid upon this is related to protection of interests and the working class value that good supervision necessitates adequate knowledge by the supervisor of the job that he is supervising. Both groups of men resented the firm's advertising for supervisory staff in the local paper. This criticism was particularly noticeable among the night men where, we remember, eight of the sample had been unsuccessful applicants in the past. 'They come in off the road, above men who have been here for years, and then of course they expect us to explain the jobs to them', was a typical response.

Again, therefore, there appears to be a harmony between both groups in their assessment of what constitutes 'good supervision'. Yet the day men were less likely to believe that the right people were chosen. This could be just a spill over of their general discontent, but seems more likely to be one of the causes of the discontent. Their perceptions tended to be less favourable than those of the night men because, it appears, their relationships with supervisors were less satisfactory.

Although the men placed much more stress than did the women upon the need for their supervisor to be technically proficient, it does not follow that the men saw 'human orientation' as being unimportant. Indeed, as we have seen, a substantial proportion of the criticisms of both groups mentioned this. When we turn to reasons for approval, we find this aspect was more often mentioned by the night shift; 20% of the night men but only 6% of the day men said either that supervision was of the 'right calibre' or that they treated the workers decently. This probably reflects an overall difference of supervisor-worker relations between shifts. On the night shift, we have seen, these relations were much less formal than on the day shift, as a result of the shift's size, social isolation from the rest of the organisation, and the level of unionisation. Also, as we saw earlier, the younger workers of both sexes tended to be more antagonistic to their supervisors, and the young men were all on the day shift. These factors, together with the fact that the night worker was less discontented with his job anyway, result in his criticism of the supervisory staff being much less dramatic than that of the day shift worker.

Own supervisor

The continuance of this differential is revealed in table 5.5. Here we see that 63% of the night workers thought their supervisor to be above average for the plant, while only half the day men thought the same. Similarly 58% of the part-time women thought their supervisor above average while 39% of the full-time women felt this way. In addition only two of the part-time women but more of the full-time women thought their supervisor to be below the average standard for the plant.

This criticism from the full-time women appeared to arise mainly in the large conveyor-belt department, Big Block, which accounted for twelve of the

Table 5.5 *How does your supervisor compare with other supervisors in the plant?*

	Day men	Night men	Full-time women	Part-time women	All
The best	12	3	17	10	42
One of the best	20	26	26	35	107
Average	28	14	48	24	114
One of the worst	3	3	13	2	21
The worst	–	–	4	–	4
Don't know	1	–	1	7	9
Total	64	46	109	78	297

seventeen responses.[4] In fact 21% of the full-time women in this department thought their supervisor was below average. There also appeared to be a tendency, though it was not significant, for the part-time women in this department to have less favourable perceptions of their supervisors. It seems probable that the size of the department was important, with its greater potential for the workers to feel isolated and hence need more 'human related' supervision. In keeping with this, those in the department who thought the right people were appointed as supervisors were more likely than in other departments to base their approval on the way the supervisors treated the women. However, we should not make too much of this size effect, since our evidence is limited due to small numbers.

The tendencies revealed in the past series of tables are substantiated by table 5.6.

The relationship between the workers and their supervision tended to be an amicable one. Most of the members of all the groups saw themselves as being on basically friendly relations with their supervisors. The men, however, seemed more likely to develop these relationships than the women – 89% of the night men, 80% of the day men, 61% of the full-time women and 64% of the part-time women indicated that their relationships with their supervisors was on a friendly basis. However, the position is not quite so straightforward.

The great majority of workers described their relations with supervisors as 'quite friendly'. This was particularly true of the night men and part-time

---

4 However, this is only significant at the 10% level.

Table 5.6 *How friendly are you with your supervisor?*

	Day men	Night men	Full-time women	Part-time women	All
Extremely friendly	10	1	12	5	28
Quite friendly	41	40	55	45	181
Indifferent	6	2	18	2	28
Not very friendly	3	1	12	2	18
Don't know each other	4	2	12	24	42
Total	64	46	109	78	297

women, who were less likely than the other groups to refer to an absence of friendliness by expressing dislike or indifference, but who were also less likely to have developed the basically friendly relationships into *close* personal ties. In both groups there was a predominantly easy-going relationship with supervisors, producing few strong feelings of friendship or hostility. In fact, 31% of the part-time women felt that they didn't really know their supervisor personally, compared with only 11% of the full-time women and as few as 4% of the night men. This further suggests that the part-time women were much less involved in their work than the other groups. Also, being older, they were treated with more respect which facilitated a relaxed atmosphere.

The night workers, on the other hand, were more involved in the firm than any other group; they saw the firm satisfying their basic work expectations. As a group, however, night men were less inclined than anyone else to desire, or obtain, highly developed friendship relations at their place of work; their involvement was basically instrumental. However, the social isolation of the night shift from the rest of the factory had led to the development of a 'night-shift culture'. One aspect of this was the unity of experience that was common to all night men. Men and supervision alike saw themselves as a race apart from the day shift. This sentiment was also prevalent on the day shift, whose attitudes were summed up by the supervisor who remarked, 'the night shift all stand along Meadow Road and crow at the break of dawn'. This remark clearly indicates the importance of the insulation of the night shift from the day shift. Perhaps the most important development in the 'night culture' was that the strict formal pattern of supervisor-worker relations of the day shift had been adapted, to some extent, into a more malleable informal relationship.[5] Although the night worker was critical of the control system, and hence of the supervision that adversely affected him in his job, the shift was more able to adapt to this situation of strain. Often, conflict situations could be reduced by uniting criticism against the day shift. Part of this informal pattern is revealed in the fact that workers on the night shift tended to have friendly relationships with both their fellow workers and their supervisors. These relationships were rarely as intense as those sometimes perceived on the day shift, but they were far more dominant.

In comparison with the night men and the part-time women, the day men and full-time women were more inclined to develop either very friendly or antagonistic relationships with their supervisors. Sixteen per cent of the day men and 11% of the full-time women said they were on extremely friendly terms with their supervisors. At the same time 9% of the day men, and 17% of the full-time women were indifferent toward their supervisors,[6] while 5% and 11% of these groups professed to be actively hostile toward them. Although these represent minority responses even in these groups, it is worth noting that over a quarter of the full-time women were relatively hostile towards their supervisors.

It is not surprising that these groups were more likely to have extreme feelings about their supervisors, as supervision tended to be more important to them. In view of their generally critical attitudes towards supervision, which we have already observed, we might have expected them to be less friendly with supervisors, and on this basis the day men would appear surprisingly unhostile. However, it has frequently been observed that criticism of supervision in general often goes with approval of the respondent's own supervisor, and that appears to have been the case here. On the other hand, the discontent of the full-time women stemmed directly from their unmet expectations concerning personal relations with the supervisors.

It will be useful to develop these points further. When the full-time women who had relatively unfriendly relationships with their supervisors were asked further questions about the relationship, the responses fell into the pattern of criticism that we have already noted. The girls valued friendly relationships with both their workmates and their supervisors. Where they were not friendly with or indifferent toward their supervisor it was usually because she was considered to be 'aloof' or 'big-headed' — she was not 'one of the girls' or she 'looked down at the girls'. It appeared continually that the girls

---

5 Cf. the difference between the relatively isolated miners and the surface workers as observed by A. W. Gouldner, *Patterns of Industrial Bureaucracy*.
6 Expressions of indifference were probably politely indicating mild antagonism. Certainly they were relatively hostile responses compared with the normal 'quite friendly'.

were demanding something more from their supervisor than a human relations expert. Part of the human relations tradition has always emphasised that 'effective leadership' needs to mix social skills with a degree of social distance.[7] The girls however seemed to demand that their supervisor act as an emissary — she should be *their* supervisor. She should be one of the girls and she should fight for *her* girls against 'them' — the people in the office who reallocated jobs; the men on nights who left the section in a mess; the maintenance men who wouldn't repair the belt quickly.

While we have given importance to the nature of the full-time women's orientation to work, and also the difference in age that existed between many of them and the supervision, these only constitute part of an explanation of the perceptions that the full-time women had of their supervision. In the earlier chapters we have pointed to the fact that these women got their greatest satisfaction at work from the social relationships that they developed within the work group. They used to 'pass the time' talking to the girls on the belt and singing to pop music on what was then Radio Caroline. Their main source of discontent stemmed from aspects of the system of control that operated in the factory and interfered with the pattern of interaction within the group. This, in part, related to the way supervisors 'treated the girls', and we have used this to explain the variation between the perceptions of the part-time and the full-time women. The supervisors tended to be more considerate in their relationships with married, part-time women, who expected less of them anyway. Further than by the attitudes of the supervision to the girls, however, the pattern of interaction within the work group was affected by decisions taken away from the work situation — these related to such things as work allocation, patterns of machine maintenance, level of bonus payments and so on. In this respect the full-time women saw a need for their interests to be represented to the makers of these decisions, and the person most able to do this was the supervisor.

This argument allows us to say something further about the relationship between the men on the night shift and their supervision. We have already pointed out that the social isolation of this shift and the absence from it of any member of higher management meant that operations on it were conducted much less formally than they were on days. Also we have noted that 74% of the night men were union members. These facts, taken together with the information that 28% of the responses from night men in table 5.3 above said that the worst thing about supervision on nights related to the

---

7 See, for example, F. E. Fielder, 'A Note on Leadership Theory'. Here Fielder concludes from a series of studies that 'leaders who perceive themselves to be more distant from their subordinates have more effective work units than those who perceive themselves to be closer to their men'.

difficulty of obtaining the compliance of workers, indicate that the workers on this shift were more able to bend the rules in their favour than were the girls who took over their jobs in the morning.

Evaluations of supervision

Tables 5.7 and 5.8 are directed at specific aspects of the supervisory role, and intended to isolate hyper-critical attitudes to the supervisory function. We can easily see that the trend of differentiation, already noted, between the main groups of the sample, is continued here.

Table 5.7   *Gourmets could run just as well without supervision*

	Day men	Night men	Full-time women	Part-time women	All
Agree	21	9	31	8	69
Disagree	40	33	78	70	221
Don't know	3	4	–	–	7
Total	64	46	109	78	297

Table 5.8   *Supervisors at Gourmets are paid too much*

	Day men	Night men	Full-time women	Part-time women	All
Agree	5	3	20	2	30
Disagree	32	26	38	30	126
Don't know	27	17	51	46	141
Total	64	46	109	78	297

We see that although the majority of each group tended to accept the necessity of a supervisory role, and many saw the payment received by occupants of such a role as being legitimate, minorities of each group rejected the supervisory function at Gourmets, almost out of hand. A third of the day men and 28% of the full-time women saw the supervisor as superfluous to the efficiency of the factory, while only 20% of the night men and 10% of the part-time women agreed with them. It should be further noted, however, that

102

large proportions of each group, although agreeing with the need for supervision, felt that too many supervisors were employed at the factory. As with the question on whether the right people are promoted, we find the pattern of day men being most apt to be critical and the part-time women at the other extreme. However, the most striking answers come again from the full-time women. In spite of the high demands they made of their supervisors, over a quarter felt the supervisors were so little help that things would be no worse without them.

The full-time women were also more likely to believe that supervisors were paid too much. Almost all the men and the part-time women who felt that they were able to comment on the payment question, felt that supervision at Gourmets was not over-remunerated. But a significant difference is found between these responses and those of the full-time women, where over a third of those expressing an opinion felt that supervisors were paid too much.

However, we should not pay too much attention to these answers since a high proportion of each group refused to comment because they did not know how much supervisors were paid. It is noticeable, nevertheless, that the percentage of 'don't knows' in this table is much lower than in response to the question on management salaries in chapter 3.

The responses to these questions are a further indication of the latent antagonism that existed between the worker and the work-process. We have already noted that this conflict tended to manifest itself more in the groups of full-time women and day men than in the other two groups. Here again the two 'antagonistic' groups, and in particular the full-time women, were in positions of greater conflict *vis-à-vis* supervision than either of the other two groups.

In the light of the analysis so far in this chapter, table 5.9 may appear surprising. There was a slight tendency to believe that supervisors were concerned about their well-being — half of the men, 55% of the full-time

Table 5.9 *Are supervisors concerned about the welfare of the workers?*

	Day men	Night men	Full-time women	Part-time women	All
Yes	32	23	60	57	172
No	30	22	49	21	122
Don't know	2	1	–	–	3
Total	64	46	109	78	297

women and 73% of the part-time women agreeing with the statement. Obviously the most interesting results here are the responses of the night men and the full-time women, whose usual positions have been reversed.

For once the night men were just as critical as those on days. Probably an explanation lies in the fact that this group had a different type of involvement in the firm from the other groups. Firstly we should recall that their isolation from the rest of the factory had produced an informal relationship between them and supervision, generally friendly but never as intense as occasionally found on the day shifts. At the same time work and family factors had combined to produce an involvement pattern whose essential basis was the 'economic utility' of the job. The night worker had probably experienced unemployment or a badly paid job in the past, he had a larger family than the day man and saw himself performing basically unrewarding work which would quite possibly be carried out with ease by a sixteen-year-old-girl when he went home. In this situation the shift became more important than the job — many night workers justified their pay, and a pay increase, by the hours they worked rather than the job they performed — and involvement became rationalised in terms of the pay and security that the firm offered them. The worker was less likely to criticise the supervisor for 'doing his job', but also he would be less likely to imbue the supervisory staff with a concern for the workers' welfare. Indeed it is possible that for these men the question had little meaning.

The involvement of the full-time women was rather different. Without the night men's family responsibilities, in many cases their work was a 'fill-in' between leaving school and the first child, and their involvement was generally less. However, we have seen that they did value the social rewards of their employment and had high expectations of their supervisors. As we saw earlier, this could lead to extreme attitudes of favourable and unfavourable natures. For them the question touched on an important issue and the responses were in keeping with the generally favourable perceptions of their own supervisors revealed earlier, while the substantial minority giving critical responses were probably conscious of supervisors' failure to meet their high expectations. Another side to these expectations was revealed when they were asked if supervisors had enough authority, as many of the full-time women felt that their supervisors did not have sufficient power to 'look after the girls' adequately. They tended to see their supervisors as being as much at the mercy of the impersonal department and work process as they were themselves.

However, we must not read too much into these figures in table 5.9. Respondents were fairly evenly divided between those who did and those who did not think supervisors had their welfare at heart. Even among the part-time women who, as we would expect, were more likely to have favourable perceptions, over a quarter didn't consider the supervisors were concerned about their welfare. In the other groups the proportions were well over 40%. But it was clear that the significance of the question varied between groups so that interpretation becomes rather conjectural.

SUMMARY

Throughout this chapter we have been concerned with examining the effects which the conflict, revealed in earlier chapters, between the worker and the work situation, including control mechanisms, had upon the relationship between the worker and supervision. We have enquired into the workers' perceptions of the supervision and their expectations of supervisory behaviour.

We noted that few of the sample had applied to be a supervisor in the past, and that those who had were dissatisfied with the selection procedure. We also noted that, apart from those who expressed no interest, the main reason given for non-application was inadequate length of service. The knowledge of the job that comes with service was seen to be the basic prerequisite for good supervision among the men, and although they felt that the supervisor should be concerned with the welfare of the workers, this expectation was never as dominant as among the women. Many workers in all groups felt that the best people were not chosen for supervisory positions. The men were more prone to attach blame to the selection procedure than the women, whose main complaint was that their supervisors did not adequately look after their interests. Thus the two groups of men tended to appraise supervision similarly, stressing competence and experience, while both groups of women were in agreement in regarding the good supervisor as one who 'looks after the girls'. Yet the day men and the full-time women were consistently more critical of their supervision than the other groups. Explanation of this has been sought in the involvement patterns of each group and the resultant expectations.

In particular, it seems clear that the demands made upon supervision by the full-time women were far more intense than those made by any other group. Because they had such high expectations in terms of personal relations, the full-time women were the most dissatisfied, but they were not entirely unsympathetic towards their supervisors. Many saw the role as unattractive and there was some feeling that the supervisors did not have enough power to do what the women expected of them. Nevertheless, there was a general tendency for them to rate their own supervisors lower than other groups, a higher proportion were antagonistic to their supervisors and a substantial minority felt that — on the crucial issue for them — their supervisors were not interested in the girls' welfare.

In contrast, the part-time women were consistently the most contented in this respect. Although they shared the full-time women's desire to be treated well, their evaluation differed for two reasons. One reason was that the supervisors actually did tend to treat them better; and the other was that, because of their lower involvement and less time spent at work, they felt less strongly and were more easily satisfied. The part-time women were generally more ready to comply with the status quo, their expectations from supervisors were less intense and so were their feelings of friendship or dislike.

For very different reasons the night men also were unlikely to have strong feelings about their supervisors. Their commitment to work was high but primarily instrumental, with limited importance given to actual work experience. At the same time the men were conscious of a night shift identity which they shared with their supervisors, and relationships were informal. This pattern of relationships was also influenced by the absence of higher management and the fact that the union was most strongly represented on the night shift. It would appear that in addition to being instrumentally involved the men on the night shift were in a stronger position to bargain over aspects of the control system than any other of the groups in the factory.

This sort of relationship between men and supervision could not easily exist on the day shift, and was not found in any department. The day men also had high commitment to work, but were generally dissatisfied. They did not share the high expectations of the full-time women with regard to personal relations, and so their discontent was directed more generally against the control system. As we would expect, they were more likely than night men to have strong feelings, and, in keeping with our earlier findings, their attitudes tended to be critical. However, when it came to assessing their own supervisors (rather than, say, the procedure through which they were chosen) their attitudes were more favourable than those of the full-time women.

6 Worker representation

In this chapter we examine the relationship between the workers at Brompton and the systems of negotiation and consultation which operated within the factory. While this means that we give particular attention to the ways in which they perceived the trade union, it should be remembered that Gourmets brought to Brompton an elaborate system of joint consultation which was an integral part of the company's tradition of 'enlightened' labour relations and welfare policies for their workers.[1] At the time of the study, the relative status of these two institutions – the consultative committees and the trade union – within the factory was a matter of some dispute. The level of union membership varied considerably within the factory[2] and the leading stewards were arguing for greater facilities from management for recruiting new members and for the collection of union dues.[3] Management on the other hand were strongly opposed to any trend toward the emergence of a 'union shop' at Brompton; they insisted on the need to protect the right of the individual to be a non-member and to bring his grievances as an individual to the attention of management.[4] The situation was further complicated by the fact that the full-time union officer responsible for the factory was in a state of almost perpetual conflict with both the shop-stewards and management at Brompton. He felt that the stewards weren't doing a good enough job, while management felt that he interfered too frequently in what they considered to be domestic matters.[5]

---

1 For an example of the ideology behind joint consultation within these types of companies, see C. G. Renold, *Joint Consultation over Thirty Years*.
2 See chapter 2.
3 They wanted new workers to be introduced to the union by a senior shop-steward during their period of induction and for management to agree to a 'check off' system with dues being deducted automatically from members' pay packets.
4 Some time after the study was completed, management decided that relations would be better if there were a 'union shop', and one was established.
5 It is interesting that while much emphasis has been placed upon the militancy of shop-stewards, the survey conducted for the Royal Commission on Trade Unions and Employers Associations by McCarthy and Parker found that 74% of Personnel Officers preferred to negotiate with shop-stewards rather than full-time officers. See W. E. J. McCarthy and S. R. Parker, *Shop Stewards and Workshop Relations*. This finding confirms that arrived at in an earlier survey; see H. A. Clegg *et al.*, *Trade Union Officers*.

The situation at Brompton was, therefore, quite complex, and we can do little more than touch the surface of it at this time. We shall, for example, make only passing reference to the interviews conducted with the shop-stewards and the information collected at the branch meetings. What we intend to do is to examine the attitudes held by workers at Brompton toward the trade union and the system of joint consultation. Obviously, attitudes toward these institutions were influenced by the workers' relationships with them. We might also expect, however, that the relationships which we have already observed between the workers and other aspects of the situation would exercise an important influence upon the worker-union relationship. So the differences we have isolated in the earlier chapters may be expected to have an appreciable bearing upon the discussion that follows.

GRIEVANCES

Before we consider the workers' relationships with the trade union it will be of interest to look at another aspect of representation more closely integrated in the firm's management structure, the complaints procedure, and the way in which workers saw themselves relating to it. We have noted that the men on the day shift and the full-time women tended to give responses which indicated a degree of tension and conflict within these groups. Accordingly it will be useful to look specifically at the workers' perceptions of conflict within the work situation. One of the ways we did this was to ask them how often they felt that they had genuine grounds for complaint while they were at work. Table 6.1 summarises the responses to this question.

Table 6.1   *Frequency of legitimate grievance*

Frequency	Day men	Night men	Full-time women	Part-time women*	All
At least 1/day	19	2	15	6	42
At least 1/week	15	7	33	8	63
At least 1/month	8	10	30	11	59
Less than 1/month	14	21	23	31	89
Never	6	5	4	22	37
No response	2	1	4	–	7
Total	64	46	109	78	297

We can observe the now familiar pattern of responses. Fifty-three per cent of the day men and 44% of the full-time women claimed that they had legitimate grounds for complaint at least once a week while less than 20% of the night men and part-time women so claimed. This would seem to confirm our argument that the work situation was experienced as a conflictful one for large proportions of the workers in the groups of day men and full-time women. We can develop this a stage further, however, by examining the extent to which the workers acted upon any complaints which they felt to be legitimate. The respondents were asked how often they took up a grievance, and the data is contained in table 6.2.

Table 6.2 *Frequency with which complaints were reported*

Frequency	Day men	Night men	Full-time women	Part-time women	All
Almost always	10	3	23	7	43
More than half of the time	8	16	23	9	56
About half of the time	24	10	19	6	59
Less than half of the time	7	9	15	14	45
Almost never	14	5	25	41	85
No response	1	3	4	1	9
Total	64	46	109	78	297

Initially we may note that the day men and the full-time women had the highest percentage of workers who almost always took up their complaints. Sixteen per cent of the day men and 21% of the full-time women claimed this while only 7% of the night men and 9% of the part-time women did likewise. The picture is changed, however, if we compare the percentages who took up over half of their complaints. If we combine the first two responses in table 6.2, and use this as an indicator of frequency we then find that 28% of the day men, 41% of the night men, 42% of the full-time women and 21% of the part-time women frequently took up their complaints. The part-time women were much less likely to complain formally, and this conclusion is supported by the fact that 53% of this group claimed that they almost never took up a complaint while only 22% of the day men, 11% of the night men and 23% of the full-time women gave this response.

109

To interpret these tables it will be useful to relate the responses in table 6.1 with those given in table 6.2. If we take a source of grievance occurring at least once a week to indicate a high frequency and also use 'more than half the time' to indicate a high level of reporting grievances we can obtain a four-cell table:

1 Frequent grievances Frequently reported	2 Frequent grievances Infrequently reported
3 Infrequent grievances Frequently reported	4 Infrequent grievances Infrequently reported

Table 6.3 presents data in such four cell tables for each of our four groups.[6]

Table 6.3 *Frequency of having and reporting grievances**

	Reported					
Grievances	Frequently	Infrequently	Total	Frequently	Infrequently	Total
	Day men			Night men		
Frequent	10	24	34	1	8	9
Infrequent	8	22	30	18	19	37
Total	18	46	64	19	27	46
	Full-time women			Part-time women		
Frequent	27	21	48	6	8	14
Infrequent	19	42	61	10	54	64
Total	46	63	109	16	62	78

* Those who were not able to estimate frequencies have been classed as 'infrequent'.

6 These simplified tables are presented for the sake of clarity. The full 5 × 5 matrices show similar patterns and the argument would be the same.

A number of interesting points arise from these data, which add depth to the differences that we have already noted to exist between the four groups of workers. The most obvious point, perhaps, relates to the part-time women. Sixty-nine per cent of the part-time women in our sample were placed in cell 4, and while large proportions of the other three groups came in this cell — 34% of the day men; 41% of night men and 39% of full-time women— they never dominated the group to the same extent. These data, therefore, confirm our impression of the women who worked part-time at Brompton, that they were unlikely to feel aggrieved and disinclined to complain. In contrast, the full-time women were the group who were most likely to have grievances which they took up. A quarter fell in cell 1, compared with 16% of the day men and under 10% for the others. A higher proportion of day men have been classed as having frequent grievances but unlike the full-time women they tended not to react by formally protesting to supervision; 38% fell in cell 2 compared with half this percentage of full-time women and less of the other groups. The night men were different again. While we noted from table 6.2 that similar proportions of the night men and the full-time women were inclined to report any grievance, we can now see that all but one of the night men who were so inclined rarely experienced such a grievance — 39% of the night men were in cell 3 compared with 17% of the full-time women.

There was a high overall tendency for respondents to be in cell 4, having few grievances and doing little about those they had. Apart from this we have seen that each group tended to fall in a different cell of table 6.3. Thus, with some simplification we may summarise the main points of interest by relating the full-time women to cell 1, the day men to cell 2, the night men to cell 3 and the part-time women to cell 4. Having done this a number of points of some importance can be made.

In the earlier chapters we have seen that the night men and the part-time women indicated quite high levels of satisfaction with their employment situation at Brompton. In keeping with this, both groups had large majorities who, as a rule, could find little cause for complaint. However, the night men were much more likely to take up any complaint that did arise. Most of the men on this shift were familiar with the stages of the grievance procedure and knew what action they would take if the lower levels of supervision failed to provide a satisfactory solution to a grievance which they wanted correcting. It seems that this familiarity with the procedure, together with the determination shown by many of the night men to utilise it, can be linked with the development of the trade union within the shift. The few men mentioning frequent grievances actually reported no more than their workmates, which seems odd unless the unreported grievances were private annoyances of low importance and the men concerned were really little different from the rest.

Clearly the low levels of recorded grievances by the night men and the part-time women conceal quite fundamental differences between the shop-floor behaviour of the workers in each of these groups. The part-time women's low involvement in work meant their expectations were low and generally satisfied by the company. Grievances were unlikely to be felt as important enough to make a fuss and there was virtually no collective organisation. The night men on the other hand, while basically satisfied with the rewards they received from working at Brompton, were much more involved in work as a life process than the women, and more inclined to relate their present 'satisfactory' situation to concessions gained from management in past struggles. The high score by the night men in cell 3 reflects the watchful attitude whereby even small problems, when they arose, were often seen as potential threats to their present position and so calling for action.

It is worth noting that these differences would not have been hinted at by a study of the technological structure of the work situation, since both groups performed a similar range of tasks within the identical physical situation. Nor can they be fully understood by reference to the prior orientations of typical workers in each of the groups. This approach fails to pay sufficient attention to variations in institutionalised forms of activity, such as the trade union organisation, within and between work situations.

The day men and full-time women have previously emerged as less satisfied than the other groups, with the day men more consistently and acutely dissatisfied. Here again we see these groups were more critical than the others, while of the two the day men tended to have grievances more frequently, as table 6.1 shows. However, when we turn to the frequency of reporting these grievances we find it is the women who usually complained, while the day men, in spite of their discontent, often did nothing. Bearing in mind that the day men were more likely to be in the union this looks rather surprising, and appears to reverse our argument for night men and part-time women. To understand this we need to look more closely at what actually went on on the shop floor. The women were nearly all working on the belts in packing and wrapping teams. They tended to be orientated toward the work group, and the social satisfactions they obtained within the group compensated for the repetitiveness of the work task. The men, on the other hand, were much more concerned about the type of work that they did. This concern was most noticeable amongst the youths, many of whom were basically dissatisfied with their first job. Also, the men were more isolated. They were socially isolated from the women, because of the conscious division between men's and women's work, and they spent much more time on their own anyway. As a result it seems girls on the packing belts were much better equipped to deal with any grievance that they felt. Other members of the work group were extremely likely to share, sympathise with and support any grievance. During the period of the field work it became obvious to the interviewer that few complaints were brought by individual women. The structure of the relationships within the work group meant that grievances which may be analytically defined as 'individual' – such as being moved from one job to another – became defined within the work group as 'collective'. It would seem that the particular situation of the men on the day shift, particularly those who serviced the belts, was such as to preclude this 'collective' support of the individual grievance. This immediately raises the question of the relationship between these workers and the trade union organisation, and at this point we can profitably turn to this problem.

THE WORKERS AND THE TRADE UNION

To begin with we should recall that unionisation varied between the groups. Seventy-four per cent of the night shift, 67% of the day men, 35% of the full-time women and 29% of the part-time women were members.

Turning to the workers' attitudes to unionism, the first thing to note is that roughly one-third of the men on both shifts, nearly half of the full-time women and over 60% of the part-time women felt that a well established trade union branch would be of little or no importance to them when deciding upon a place of employment. In addition to this, 41% of the day men, 20% of the night men, 33% of the full-time women and 18% of the part-time women, thought that the branch of the trade union at Gourmets was below average for the area, while a further 29% and 50% of the two groups of women felt unable to comment on the merits of their union branch.

These figures reveal immediately that the relationships of the earlier chapters are well in evidence here. The men were more highly involved in their jobs than the women, and more likely to see a trade union as being an important feature of any future work situation. The part-time women, who were much less involved than their full-time counterparts, saw a branch as being unimportant but were also unlikely to be critical of the branch at Gourmets. Similarly the night men, who were much more satisfied with their job situation than the day men, were also much more satisfied with their trade union branch, 43% of them thinking it to be above average for the area.

Criticism of, and antagonism toward the branch tended to be concentrated among the day men and the full-time women. In the latter group the women of Big Block appeared much more critical than those of the other departments.

Workers in these two groups, although differing in their involvement patterns, have been continually more critical of the control systems than the workers in the other groups. Both these groups revealed a level of discontent which was never obvious in the other groups, and it would appear from these initial responses that the union appeared to them as a further aspect of an antagonistic work situation. At first sight it seems that the trade union was linked in the minds of the workers at Brompton with other features of control that operated within the factory.

Before we take this argument further, it is important to point out that, while it is possible to relate these perceptions of the trade union to the orientations to work of the Brompton workers, taken by itself this is an inadequate explanation. It should be appreciated that the trade union itself, and hence the workers' actual experience of it, varied between the four groupings. An example of this institutional variation is found in the fact that the night shift had a higher shop-steward – worker ratio (1:50) than the day-shift men (1:58) or the groups of women (1:300).[7] This parallels the variation in union membership, with almost three-quarters of the night men and two-thirds of the day men but only about a third of the women in the union. These variations may be related to the orientations of the workers – for example the importance they attached to trade unionism – but the orientations related to specific concrete situations. In other words, while men do in a very real sense make their own history, they do not make it under circumstances that they have chosen for themselves.[8] While it is extremely important to examine the orientations which workers bring into a work situation, it should not be forgotten that the work situation has a structure which exists, in a sense, independently of those orientations. The trade union organisation forms a part of this structure, so an outline of how the situation had developed in the plant is needed in order to understand how the Brompton workers felt about trade unionism.

---

7 There were no part-time women who served as shop-stewards. The eight women stewards were full-time workers, each of whom represented some part-time workers. It is interesting to note that six of these were single and between the ages of 20 and 30. This might be taken as a further indication that during this period single women begin to think less of the day they will get married and give greater significance to their employment situation.

8 K. Marx, *The Eighteenth Brumaire of Louis Bonaparte*, p. 10, 'Men make their own history but they do not make it just as they please; they do not make it under circumstances chosen by themselves, but under circumstances directly encountered, given and transmitted from the past'.

Development of unionism at Brompton – 'the men's affair'

The unionisation of the workers at Brompton had begun amongst the men; the impetus coming in the first instance from the men on the night shift. This was predictable and can be explained in terms of the greater centrality given to work in the lives of the men and concomitantly their previous involvement with the traditions of trade unionism. Given this, however, the unionising process within the Brompton factory had consequences for the ways in which men and women related to the trade union.

Roy,[9] among others, has indicated that the union organising campaign within a factory entails quite severe tensions between workers and management and also among workers, and he shows how the campaign involves a number of dedicated active trade unionists within the factory organising support with which to confront management. This process was in evidence in the Brompton factory, where the senior stewards were concerned to obtain a union shop. Shop-stewards were sponsored by these senior stewards – a potential steward being someone who either took an immediate interest in the union when he arrived or who came into the foreground during a sectional dispute. The potential steward was appraised in terms of his dedication to developing a union organisation in the factory and the main demand upon him was that he obtained full membership on his section.

This process at Brompton was complicated by the presence of the women. The senior stewards firmly believed that the women could not be organised. Most of the men supported this view and justified it by the claim that the women either worked for 'pin money'[10] or were waiting around to get married. This belief had its greatest consequence upon the trade union organisation on the night shift. Here, in combination with the relatively high level of union membership achieved on the shift and the identification of their work as 'women's work', this belief in the fact that women could not be organised reinforced the social isolation of the shift that we have already noted.

An example of the consequences of such isolation is demonstrated by a strike that took place during the summer of our field work. The company had employed students for the summer holidays, and some of these had been put on the night shift. These students were under the age of 21 and so were not paid the full night-shift rate. The shop-stewards had long understood

---

9 D. F. Roy, 'The Union-Organising Campaign as a Problem of Social Distance'.
10 This assumption is called into question by the data we have presented.

115

that no-one under the age of 21 would be employed on the night shift. The issue was a complicated one and was seen by the stewards to have far-reaching implications. 'The thin edge of the wedge' was frequently mentioned. While we cannot, at this time, examine the strike in any detail, we can fruitfully relate two of the main tactics adopted by the night-shift stewards which were strongly supported by the men. The first related to the students. It was seen to be important for the students to realise that the strike was not against them. In fact this feeling was an important reason for the strike being articulated in terms of 'full rate for all night-shift workers'. This slogan served to unite the interests of both the night-shift workers and the students. The second tactic was of more fundamental importance. Although the issue could be seen as one which potentially affected all workers at Brompton, and although a number of stewards on the day shift emphasised this and indicated that they could 'pull a strike in support of the night shift', the night-shift stewards insisted that it was a 'night-shift affair', and that 'we can handle it better ourselves'.[11] These two tactics taken together are interesting. The stewards on the night shift were able to argue that it was important that the students appreciated the issues involved. They were all extremely pleased when a representative of the students addressed a strike meeting and expressed strong support and approval of the strike. The senior steward on the night shift recounted this event on a number of occasions, pointing out how the action itself was important as it fostered a greater understanding between students and workers. In spite of this, however, the men and shop-stewards on the night shift were not prepared to see the situation as one in which the support of the women could be obtained. There was no attempt made to 'open the eyes of the women' or even to keep the women informed of events. During the two days of the strike the interviewer casually discussed the strike with several women, none of whom had any idea of what was involved.

While it is important that too much is not drawn from this particular example, it does indicate the extent to which the 'image' of women held by the men in general and the night-shift stewards in particular affected the way in which the union developed at Brompton. Granted that women tend to be less involved in work and less committed to a trade union, the fact of the men organising themselves had further consequences for the relationship between the women and the union. For the women the union became 'the men's affair'. No women attended the branch meeting. Even the women

---

11 During this period the stewards on the night shift were continually telling stories of how the shift had restricted output in the past, and as a result successfully obtained concessions from management.

116

stewards insisted that the branch was the place where the men discussed things. It can be seen, therefore, that the belief in the inability of women to be committed union members can take on elements of a self fulfilling prophecy. Once the involvement of women is so defined by the men who organise and increase their power, the definition becomes sustained through its institutionalisation. It will be useful during this chapter to examine some of the consequences of this process and to question the validity of the particular image of women workers adhered to by the union organisers at Brompton.

Before we look at this in any detail it will be of interest to look further at the way the workers perceived their union by considering their reasons for joining or not joining.

Reasons for joining or not joining

Once we had established whether or not respondents were in the union, the first question we asked of members, which specifically related to trade unionism, was 'How did you come to join the trade union at Brompton?' Non-members were asked whether there was a specific reason why they hadn't joined. The responses are presented in table 6.4.

A high proportion of all union members stressed ideological reasons for joining the union.[12] Over half the men, 32% of the full-time women, and 43% of the part-time women members gave responses of this type. In general these responses laid stress upon the need for the worker to rely upon collective action. Frequently they were loosely formulated: 'You need a union don't you'; 'We'd get no-where without a union – I've always been a union man'; – but occasionally members were more explicit. 'The unions have got the worker everything that he's got today. Above all they've given him his self respect. I'd say a lot of things against them – especially this one here – but we just couldn't think of being without one. A bad union is better than no union at all' was a response from an operator on the day shift. Responses of this order indicate the influence of working-class history and tradition in the area. Membership is precipitated by wider considerations than the position of the individual worker in the firm; it draws upon the whole history of experience shared by the worker, his family and his class.

On a more instrumental level we have the 'business unionist' response. Unlike the ideological union member, the business unionist tends to stress the

---

12 The wording of the question was designed to avoid forcing ideological responses, by referring to the event rather than to attitudes as in the usual question 'Why . . .'. It is interesting that when a similar question was asked of bank clerks very few gave ideological responses. See R. M. Blackburn, *Union Character and Social Class*, pp. 208-9.

Table 6.4   *Reasons for membership – non-membership of the union*

Union members

	Day men	Night men	Full-time women	Part-time women	All
'Ideological' unionist	22	18	12	10	62
'Business' unionist	7	4	6	1	18
Problem	2	2	6	–	10
Everyone else joined	7	9	10	10	36
Asked to join	5	1	3	1	10
Other	–	–	1	1	2
Total	43	34	38	23	138

Non-members

	Day men	Night men	Full time women	Part-time women	All
Anti-trade union ideology	4	1	1	6	12
This union is no good	3	2	14	4	23
Ex-member	8	7	18	4	37
Never been asked	4	1	17	25	47
No need to join	–	–	17	12	29
Other	2	1	4	4	11
Total	21	12	71	55	159

economic advantages that he, as an individual, receives by virtue of his union membership. Strike pay, insurance, sick benefits, were all quoted here, together with the protection that the union could give him in his job. Thirteen per cent of the membership gave this type of response. With these we may link a further 7% who joined because of some specific individual problem. There is, of course, a point where 'business unionism' in the form of collective means to individual ends merges with ideological unionism, with a common stress on collective solidarity, but it is generally meaningful to distinguish quite sharply the practical reasons from the ideological.

Reasons for membership appear similar for all groups, except for a tendency for ideological considerations to be of greater importance to the men while the women were more susceptible to social pressures. Nearly half the part-time women and a third of the full-time women joined because the other members of the work group joined, or because they were asked by a shop-steward. On the other hand, only a quarter of the men had joined for these reasons. This trend is also revealed in the proffered reasons for non-membership; the women, particularly the part-time women, were far more likely to say that they had not joined because they had never been asked.[13]

When we look more closely at this pattern among the Brompton workers, we find it was not so much a result of different orientations of men and women as of previous contact with unions.[14] Only three of the women were union members in their last place of employment (each of these had been a member of the U.S.D.A.W. branch at the local Co-op) and almost all of the rest had not been working where unions were available; in fact many of the women were either school leavers or housewives and only a handful of them had prior experience of factory work. Large proportions of the men, however, had been previously employed in unionised work situations. In fact 41% of the day men (even though a quarter of all the day men were school leavers) and 59% of the night men had been members of a union in their last place of employment. Given this distinction it is instructive to examine in detail the men who quoted social reasons for their membership or non-membership of the union at Brompton. Sixteen of the day men and eleven of the night men either joined for 'social reasons' or claimed that they had never been asked to join the branch at Brompton. Of the eleven night men, only two had been union members previously; one had decided not to pay his dues at Brompton because he 'hadn't been asked', while the other claimed to have joined because his mate, who moved to the plant with him, intended to continue with his membership. Of the remaining nine workers, four had been previously employed as clerical workers, another four as retail workers and the remaining one as an unskilled manual worker. A similar pattern is revealed in the sixteen day men who indicated social reasons. Here only one man was a

---

13 The tendency is not significant for members alone, but is for non-members, and when reasons for membership and non-membership are combined it is highly significant (p <0·001).
14 This tendency for women to be more influenced by social factors has been noted in a different work situation, where unlike Brompton, previous union contact was not relevant since virtually no-one had any previous employment. Cf. R. M. Blackburn, *Union Character and Social Class*, pp. 209-10.

member when he arrived, nine were school-leavers and the remaining six divided evenly between clerical and retail workers. The pattern is a definite one. Men who gave social reasons for joining or not joining the trade union tended to be those who had had little or no direct experience of trade unionism before they came to the plant. Men who had had a past experience of union membership were much more inclined to give definite, specific reasons for joining the union at Brompton.[15] This relationship between responses and union background suggests quite dramatically that attitudes toward trade unionism tend to be hardened and made specific by the direct experience of trade unions at work.

This relationship may help to explain the fact that 23% of the women non-members thought that there was 'no need' to join the union at Brompton. However, the fact that none of the men gave this response is also important. This points further to the fact that for the women involvement in the employing organisation centred around the work group, and the union at Brompton had little influence upon these groups. Only a minority had been recruited so any contextual effect would not encourage belief in the union's importance, and as we noted earlier there was a tendency among men and women to see union matters as men's affairs.

It is important to appreciate that there were quite fundamental differences in the types of responses given by the two groups of women. Our previous analysis would lead us to expect that although similar proportions of both groups were members of the union, the full-time women would be more likely to give specific criticisms of the union as reasons for their non-membership. This in fact was the case — 45% of the full-time women who were not members of the union quoted specific discontents with the union organisation at Brompton as the main reason for not joining, or not continuing as members of the union. Over half of these — a quarter of the non-members — were ex-members who were almost all extremely critical of the union. In responding to the questions on the trade union, the full-time women who were critical of the union were often extremely articulate and answered the questions at much greater length than they answered many of the others they were asked. This was particularly the case in the large packing block — Big Block — where a number of the work groups had staged walk-outs recently over errors, or suspected errors, in the calculation of their pay under

---

15 This doesn't mean that members will not leave a union under any circumstances. The knife seems to cut both ways, for six of the men 'Ex-members' were members on arrival. All had left the union, at least in part, because it compared badly with branch organisations they had experienced in the past.

the newly introduced 'grading system'. It is worth looking at a rather large sample of the responses to demonstrate this point:

'We went on strike over "waiting time". We didn't gain a thing. The union wouldn't help us. He just told us to go' back to work. Just like a foreman he was. It doesn't seem like a union here. They do nothing for you. They're all talk – they just keep putting things off.'

'They don't seem to do much for us. They don't seem to be for the workers; they're more on the firm's side. You need to have *good* people in charge of the union. These here – they just talk round the questions you put to them – you never get a straight answer.'

'They don't do anything for the girls. I went to the strike meeting that they had – they just tied you up in knots. They'll do nothing until you walk out of the building. You need to do something pretty drastic before they'll take any notice. They've lost an awful lot of members. The union here is in Gourmets' pocket.'

'They don't do a lot for you. Most of the time they do nothing. I left – we all left together – because of the night men. We were sick and fed up of the state they left the belt for us to come in to in the morning. The union man did nothing. Apparently he was laughing at us.'

'The union here is just a waste of time. I can't see what it's supposed to be doing. Two or three of us just dropped out. It was a waste of time. You complain and they do nothing about it. We went to the table (the senior stewards sat at a 'union table' in the canteen) about a dozen times once and they did nothing for us.'

'I didn't mind joining in the Co-op. It was a strong union there; it does something for you. Here, they back down when management look at them. I'd begrudge paying my half a crown a week to this lot.'

Compared with these responses from the full-time women the part-time women were quite mild. In fact a much smaller proportion of the part-time women were at all critical. The critical responses taken together with the ex-members only amounted to 15% of the non-members. As we would expect, among the men the proportion of non-members expressing specific criticisms was even higher than among the full-time women.[16] However, these men were

---

16 Because the proportion in both cases was fairly large, the difference was not significant.

substantially fewer in relation to the number of members. Almost four times as many men were members as explained non-membership on grounds of disapproval of the union, whereas the full-time women members barely outnumbered the critics. Similarly the ratio of members to ex-members was about 5:1 for the men and 2:1 for the full-time women. Looking at it another way, of all the non-members who quoted these critical types of response, over half were full-time women.

The relationship between the worker and the union, therefore, tended to be closely associated with the patterns we have developed in the previous chapters. The part-time woman, because of her lower involvement, was likely to be neutral toward the union. The night man, because of his general satisfaction with his economic rewards and the more flexible organisation of the night shift (itself related to the development of the union on the shift), was likely to be more involved in, and less critical of the union than other groups. However, the day men and full-time women, although revealing different types and degrees of involvement, were much more likely to be critical of this aspect of the control system than the other two groups. A particularly large percentage of the full-time women were severely critical of the union and often gave this as a reason for non-membership. The day men on the other hand were less inclined to take this criticism to the extent of not joining or of leaving the union.

Commitment to unionism

In table 6.5 we have widened the discussion to a consideration of trade unionism in general, rather than as a specific feature of the individual's work experience. Here workers were asked to consider whether or not all workers should be in a trade union. This question attempts to get at the worker's attitude toward unionism as a principle rather than as an aspect of his present job.

The dramatic feature of this table is that the majority of the sample, members (86%) and non-members (74%) alike, believed that all workers should be in a union. A few of the non-members felt that unions were a bad thing, while rather more of both members and non-members argued that the individual should be free to please himself about membership. In general, however, the replies expressed a marked pro-union ideology.

Somewhat surprising is the large proportion of women who thought that all workers should be union members. About three-quarters of them expressed this view, with hardly any difference in the proportions of members and non-members. In contrast, among the men the members were significantly more likely to answer that all workers should be in a union, as many as 92% supporting this view, compared with 70% of

Table 6.5 *Should all workers be members of a union?*

Members

	Day men	Night men	Full-time women	Part-time women	All
YES:					
Working man needs a union	18	17	15	8	58
Worker more powerful	9	6	6	6	27
No point 50/50	6	–	6	1	13
Non-members benefit	6	9	1	4	20
	39	32	28	19	118
NO:					
Free to choose	4	2	10	4	20
All members	43	34	38	23	138

Non-members

	Day men	Night men	Full-time women	Part-time women	All
YES:					
Working man needs a union	3	3	16	19	41
Worker more powerful	10	3	18	12	43
No point 50/50	1	3	15	12	31
	14	9	49	43	115
NO:					
Free to choose	3	1	13	3	20
No need for unions	4	2	9	9	24
	7	3	22	12	44
All non-members	21	12	71	55	159

123

non-members. Indeed the proportion of male non-members was slightly (though not significantly) lower than the proportion of women non-members, though the position was clearly reversed for members. Among members it is possible that the greater readiness of the women to say workers should be free to choose was due to a reluctance to imply criticism of their many workmates outside the union.[17] Nevertheless, the overall feeling was one of positive support for unions.

An interesting example of the lower involvement of the part-time woman was revealed here, when many of this group answered that they thought all workers should be in a union, but not part-time women. Some of the part-time women, it seems, did not perceive themselves as being 'workers'.

A relationship between the workers' work experience and assessment of unionism is further revealed by the fact that large numbers of women felt that unionism was a good thing, 'because there is no point being half in and half out'. A typical response of this type was given by an 18 year old packer who was not a union member.

'If there's got to be a trade union everyone should be in it. There's no point being half in and half out, that just leads to ill feeling. We all need to be united then we'd be more powerful. Even on some of the belts you've got some girls in and some of them out. That's not right!'
This type of response is almost certainly related to the increase in the conflict potential that is caused within the work group when some of the women are members and some are not. In this context it is significant that many of the women members joined the union as a direct result of social pressure.

Commitment to the union at Brompton
Many of the responses, however, reveal a dichotomy between the workers' relationship with the union branch at Gourmets and trade unionism in general. We have already mentioned the part-time women who 'opted out'; many other respondents indicated that although they were in favour of trade unionism in general they saw little point in joining the branch at the firm. Further indication of this trait is revealed in table 6.6.

---

17 Sami Dassa, 'L'analyse contextuelle appliquée aux orientations et aux comportements syndicaux', observes that contextual influences on orientations towards unionism operate mainly on union *members*, who tend to be pro-union. This may explain the pattern here; the highly unionised male context had no influence on non-members and the members tended to be more pro-union, but among the women who were predominantly non-members the contextual effect reduced members' pro-union orientations to the level of the non-members. See also table 6.7.

Table 6.6 *How would you feel if the trade union were unable to continue at Gourmets?*

Response	Day men	Night men	Full-time women	Part-time women	All
Very badly	25	25	15	14	79
Quite badly	11	6	37	14	68
Wouldn't mind all that much	12	8	19	23	62
Wouldn't mind at all	15	7	27	14	63
Be pleased	1	–	–	–	1
Don't know	–	–	11	13	24
Total	64	46	109	78	297

Because of their lower involvement in the union, about 13% of the women were unable to say how they would feel in the hypothetical situation of the union being unable to continue. Of all groups, the men on the night shift would feel most badly about the absence of the union – two-thirds of them would feel either badly or very badly, while 56% of the day men, 48% of the full-time women, and 36% of the part-time women would feel the same.

A number of the respondents who gave these committed responses justified them in strong ideological terms. One man on the night shift, for example, replied, 'What! . . . If the union packed up, I'd pack up.' Others, mostly among the men, insisted likewise – they wouldn't wish to work in any place where there was no union organisation. More typical, however, were responses which stressed the ambivalent nature of commitment to the union at Brompton. A number of responses will make this point more explicit.

A 40-year-old male operator on day shift.

'The branch here is not a lot of good, but I'd hate to think what would happen without it. They'd have a field day. The whip would really come out then.'

A 53-year-old belt worker on the night shift.

'At least there's some protection if you're in a union. They could do all sorts if there was no union. They could go all the way home.'

A 17-year-old packer.

> 'Well this one don't do a lot for you, but it's better than nothing. They are at least *supposed* to be for the workers. I think we'd be worse off without one at all.'

It is important to note that the committed men on the night shift were much less likely to give such ambivalent responses than their counterparts in the other three groups. Frequently these men replied that 'the union has got us what we've got out of this company' and that the union was important as it 'kept the men together' and prevented management from 'getting it all their own way'.

A large proportion of all four groups, therefore, believed in a trade union ideology, and were positively committed to the trade union organisation at Brompton, while the commitment of the night men appears much more definite than that observed in the other three groups. Although workers may have been critical of their own branch, frequently this criticism was tempered by the belief that some form of union organisation is essential as a check upon the indiscriminate use of power by management. It is of further interest in this respect that no respondents made specific reference to the 'instrumental rewards' of union membership in justifying their commitment to the union.

On the other hand, it is important not to lose sight of the fact that a substantial proportion of our four groups would clearly not grieve the departure of the union from the Brompton factory. If we take the bottom four responses in table 6.6 to indicate a lack of positive commitment to the union (i.e., including those who answered 'don't know') we find that 33% of the night men, 44% of the day men, 52% of the full-time women and 64% of the part-time women lacked such a commitment. Of the respondents who showed least attachment to the union — those who 'wouldn't mind at all' and the one man who would actually be pleased — two-thirds came from the full-time women and the day men.

Many of the uncommitted respondents had previously indicated a firm belief in the principle of trade unionism and, in keeping with this, few of them justified their responses with anti-unionist beliefs. The most frequent replies were either rather neutral ones which claimed that they were unsure of what the union did, but that it hadn't had much effect upon their lives and so they couldn't see how they would miss it, or, less frequently, full-blooded criticisms of the trade union organisation as it existed in the plant. As we would expect, these latter responses were most likely to come from the full-time women and the day men, the women again tending to be most forthright. Typical comments of this sort were:

> 'They are no good . . . no bloody good at all. For all the good they do they'd better pack up. I wouldn't miss them.'

'It would be different if they did something. I've told you though, they don't. They do nothing. I can't see what difference it would make if they left. Except to them that is.'

These responses again, therefore, tend to confirm the pattern that we have noted throughout this, and earlier chapters. It will be useful to examine further the responses recorded in table 6.6 by relating them to union membership. Taking the first two responses – that they would feel badly or very badly – as indications of commitment and the others as indicating no commitment, we get the distributions of table 6.7.

Table 6.7 *Commitment to the union at Brompton by membership*

| Commitment | Membership | | | | | |
	Members	Non-members	Total	Members	Non-members	Total
	Day men			Night men		
Positive	29	7	36	26	5	31
None	14	14	28	8	7	15
Total	43	21	64	34	12	46
	Full-time women			Part-time women		
Positive	23	29	52	11	17	28
None	15	42	57	12	38	50
Total	38	71	109	23	55	78

The most striking thing about this table is the low association between commitment and membership. To be sure it is always in the expected direction, but is very weak among the women, and even among the men it is fairly low – phi = 0·33 for night men and 0·32 for day men.[18] What this means is that attitudes towards the union were only poorly related to actual membership. The implications of this are twofold, as indicated by the

---

18 The relationship is not even significant for the two groups of women taken separately, though it is when they are taken together. In each case phi < 0·2. The lower association for the women is mainly due to lower commitment among women members, which is again consistent with the contextual effect noted by Dassa. (See note 17, p. 124.)

substantial proportions in the two discrepant cells — the top right and bottom left corners — for each group. Firstly we see that quite large proportions of the union membership in the plant lacked any firm commitment to the union organisation. This is most noticeable amongst the groups of women but a third of the union members among the day men also lacked such a commitment. Secondly, many of those who expressed a commitment to the union organisation were not union members. This was particularly so in the two groups of women, where only a minority of those who expressed a commitment to the union at Brompton were in fact members of the union. This bears out our earlier evidence suggesting that the women workers at Brompton were a much more fruitful source of union members than the recruitment strategy of the union organisation would lead us to expect. We see that, unlike the men, they were more likely to be positively committed than to be members.

Thus the low relationship between membership and attitudes to the union was the result of two factors. The general dissatisfaction with the union was coupled with a widespread belief in the need for a union so that, as we have seen, some workers joined on principle without any commitment to their particular union while others were unwilling to join but nevertheless felt the union was necessary. On top of this conflict between ideology and immediate experience was the belief that the union was the men's affair. This meant that more women, with favourable attitudes, could have been recruited.

THE SHOP-STEWARDS

We have previously argued that concrete experience of trade union activity within the factory situation has an important influence upon the attitudes that workers hold toward trade unions. In the Brompton plant, however, there was tension between the workers' generalised understanding of unionism and their concrete experience of it in the work place. So it is important to examine further the specific nature of the relationship between the workers and their union. Frequently we found that criticisms of the trade union were similar to those directed at supervision. 'The union' made little attempt to look after the workers, it was on 'their side'. Now Peck,[19] amongst others, has pointed out that for the rank and file union member the union often becomes identified with the local levels of leadership. Accordingly we must look at perceptions of the branch officials and the shop stewards.

All in all there were thirty-one stewards in the plant; eleven on the night shift and twelve men and eight women on the day shift. The company refused

19 S. M. Peck, *The Rank-and-File Leader.*

to recognise a convener[20] but the branch secretary — a night shift worker who was employed on the lowest grade of work — acted as the senior steward in the factory. In effect he acted as a *de facto* convener without receiving the usual privileges of the position; he remained an ordinary worker on the night shift. This frequently meant that he had to come back into the plant on the day shift in order to take part in negotiations with management. The branch chairman acted as the senior steward of the day shift.

The stewards on the day shift tended to be significantly older and have a lengthier service with the company than their members. However, this relationship did not hold on the night shift; if anything the opposite was the case, the stewards having the same mean length of service as the membership but a mean age four years younger than that of the members. Similarly over half the night stewards — six — were belt workers, while only a third of the men and a quarter of the women stewards on days worked in such jobs. As we are dealing in such small numbers, any inference that we draw from them will need to be supported by further evidence, but it seems reasonable to suggest that the stewards on the night shift, in terms of such basic characteristics as age, length of service and job type were closer to the membership than their counterparts on the day shift.

Each shop-steward was responsible for a particular area of the factory. However, many workers, especially among the women, had no such sectional steward. These workers were represented in a dispute by the senior steward on the day shift, and they would pay their dues during meal breaks at the union table in the canteen. For many of the workers this union table was their main contact with the trade union.

As a minimal measure of their relationships with their steward, all respondents, both members and non-members were asked if they could name the shop-steward who was responsible for the area of the factory where they worked. In addition to Yes and No responses we have recorded a category termed 'wrong answer'. Too much should not be read into this response, it simply indicates that workers named a steward other than the one whom the interviewer knew to be responsible for the respondents particular work situation. Almost invariably these respondents named one of the senior stewards. It can be seen from table 6.8 that only just over half of the workers in our sample knew who their shop-steward was. Perhaps the most interesting feature of the table, however, is the fact that 42% of the day men were unable

---

20 One of the main points of conflict in any discussion of this topic between management and the union was the level of union membership in the plant. Our sample estimate in fact falls between the figures usually quoted by the two sides.

Table 6.8   *Whether shop-steward known*

	Day men	Night men	Full-time women	Part-time women	All
Yes	34	34	56	26	150
'Wrong answer'	3	6	9	6	24
No	27	6	44	46	123
Total	64	46	109	78	297

to give an answer. Of all the groups, the day men are the only one in which the number of respondents who gave a negative response to this question exceeded the number of non-members in the group. Bearing in mind the distribution of union members within the groups it is rather surprising that only the part-time women were less well informed, and even there only 59% could not answer compared with 71% who were non-members. On the other hand the low proportion of night men (13%) who failed to name a steward is just what we would expect. This information appears to give further support to the arguments that the day men experienced considerable social isolation while at work and that the women had greater interest in the union than their membership figures suggest.

The workers who were able to name a shop-steward were asked how often they had cause to see him on matters that related to the trade union. It was pointed out that such matters might cover grievances relating to pay, working

Table 6.9   *Contact with shop-steward on union business*

	Day men	Night men	Full-time women	Part-time women	All
At least once a day	–	3	2	–	5
Once a week	6	8	7	4	25
Once a month	3	6	16	2	27
Less than once a month	10	17	23	7	57
Almost never	18	6	17	19	60
Total	37	40	65	32	174

conditions and the like, as well as aspects of union administration. These responses continue the pattern we noted in the previous table. The groups are clearly ordered, with the night-shift workers having most contact with shop-stewards, followed by full-time women, day men and part-time women. This is perhaps most clearly seen in the proportions with virtually no contact − 15% of night men, a quarter of full-time women, half the day men and 59% of part-time women − though the differences are also observable at more frequent rates of contact. Not surprisingly we find that the two groups where workers were most likely to report their complaints regularly also had large proportions who frequently contacted their shop steward on 'union issues'. It is noticeable, however, that the frequency with which all respondents contact their steward is lower than their reported level of grievances. Furthermore, apart from the night shift, the frequency with which workers met their shop-steward appeared lower at Brompton than in other work situations that have been studied.[21]

When we relate contact with stewards to union membership the contrast is again between the full-time women and the men of the day shift. The former was the only group where there were more who saw their stewards at least sometimes than there were members; among the day men the number was less than half the number of members. Below the full-time women were the night men, with equal numbers, and even the part-time women came clearly above the day men.

Central to the way workers relate to their stewards is their perception of the role of the shop-steward in the factory. In this context each of the respondents was asked what he or she considered to be the main attractions and the main drawbacks associated with the position of shop-steward.

The first thing to note is the much higher proportion of women (well over a third) who felt unable to answer the question. These responses relate more simply to our initial contention of work being more central in the lives of men ¿han women. It also links with the pattern of union membership, and we find that thirty of the full-time women and twenty-four of the part-time women who answered that they 'didn't know' were not members of the union.

We should note that the majority of the responses recorded by each group implied that the shop-steward's role had a number of attractions which were seen to be legitimate by the respondents. Nearly 40% of the day men and full-time women, and 26% from the night men and the part-time women saw

---

21 E.g. Goldthorpe *et al.*, *The Affluent Worker: Industrial Attitudes and Behaviour*, p. 106, found 30% saw their steward on union related issues 'a good deal'.

Table 6.10 *Main attractions of being a shop-steward**

Response	Day men		Night men		Full-time women		Part-time women	
	No.	%	No.	%	No.	%	No.	%
Help workmates	25	39	12	26	41	38	20	26
Interesting job	10	16	8	17	15	14	21	27
Status†	5	8	11	24	6	6	10	13
Out for themselves†	19	30	11	24	6	6	5	6
Other	9	14	2	4	7	6	3	4
Nothing	7	11	6	13	9	8	7	9
Don't know	9	14	4	9	39	36	30	38
Total	84	131	54	117	123	113	96	123

* Respondents were allowed two responses to this question, see table 3.2.
† This distinction between 'status' and 'out for themselves' is similar to the one made between 'status' and 'ego satisfaction', in the chapter on supervision. See in particular table 5.3.

that the position of shop-steward could be used to help the workers. In addition to this, appreciable proportions of each of the groups saw that the shop-steward's job would be an interesting one which carried a certain amount of status within the factory. Perhaps the most surprising thing here is the fact that 50% of the responses given by the full-time women – and in fact 74% of the responses other than 'don't know' – implied an appreciation of quite legitimate rewards received by shop-stewards.[22] This finding is all the more surprising when we remember that this group of women, in addition to being harshly critical of both the trade union and supervision in the factory, were also the most likely to question the motives and the legitimacy of supervisors. When we examine the distribution of responses which imply a criticism of shop-stewards – that they are 'out for themselves' or that they are just after an easy time – we find that only 6% of the full-time women made such comments as compared with 30% of the day men and 24% of the night men, though they differed little from the part-time women.

22 Though the proportion of respondents was a little lower in each case.

It is obvious that the number of responses which imply a criticism of the shop-steward role within the factory is much lower than the number which implied such a criticism of the supervisory role. The distribution of criticism deserves some comment however. One possible explanation can be found in the particular way in which the trade union developed within the factory at Brompton so that far greater pressure was likely to be directed against men who were not in the union than women non-members. This pressure might help explain the fact that while most of the women non-members gave sympathetic responses or answered 'don't know' to the question of shop-steward satisfaction, many of the men non-members were inclined to give a critical response. Of the thirty men who claimed that shop-stewards were 'out for themselves', fourteen were non-members. This means that non-members were twice as likely as members to give critical answers, 42% doing so compared with 21% of members among these men. At the same time it is relevant to recall the collective approach to taking up the individual grievances of the full-time women, which might blur perceptions of the shop-steward's role but would help to show it as a supportive role.

Of further interest here are the answers given by union members when asked if they were interested in standing for the position of shop-steward. Only two of the night men and one of the part-time women expressed any such interest, while seven of the day men and thirteen of the full-time women (34% of the membership) answered likewise. All of the day men and the full-time women who were interested in becoming a shop-steward said that their interest stemmed from the fact that they would be able to help their workmates. Eight of the full-time women in fact added that they would only stand if they were asked to do so by their mates. A similar attitude was reflected by six of the eight women stewards who claimed that their election was prompted by 'the girls on the belt'.

If we turn now to the reasons given for lack of interest in holding the office we find that while majorities of the day men and women gave 'apathetic type' answers — they 'weren't interested', or they 'only paid their dues' — 62% of the night men who didn't want office claimed that the job of shop-steward was basically unattractive and 43% of the women members explained their lack of interest in terms of their lack of ability — they considered themselves ill-equipped to perform the role.

While none of these observations is in itself particularly illuminating — again we are dealing in small numbers — taken together they seem to fall into a now recognisable pattern. The full-time women felt strongly that there was a need for someone to represent the girls' interests, and saw a great deal of satisfaction to be obtained by anyone who was able to do so. Consequently they were more inclined to see the steward's job as attractive, but this attraction was dependent upon support from the girls on the belt. Many of the women members who were not interested in the office, explained their reasons not in terms of apathy or the unattractive nature of the job but rather by claiming that they didn't have the ability and so might 'let everyone down'.

The day men also felt strongly that they needed someone to represent their interests. They did not share the women's social expectations, but they were frequently placed in a job situation which they felt to be profoundly unsatisfactory and were often socially isolated. They had relatively little contact with the shop-stewards. Many felt that they were inadequately represented but there was little they could do about it. The system of representation was established and run by the men, and although there was considerable feeling that they ran it badly there was little scope for change. To change it would entail opposing the system and the existing representatives. Such opposition requires certain political skills and a degree of social support, and the day men — particularly the younger ones — were likely to be lacking in both.

The night men's responses are perhaps more difficult to understand and before we make such an attempt it will be useful to examine the information contained in table 6.11. We can readily see there was a large amount of agreement that the worst thing associated with the shop-steward's role is the bad relationships which can develop between the steward and the workers. It is of interest that this was also seen as the main drawback faced by supervisors. Although this response tends to be the largest single one in each of the four groups, it is most noticeable amongst the night men, and in least evidence among the full-time women. The number of full-time women who mentioned potential conflicts with workers is strikingly low, even allowing for the large proportion who were unable to answer the question. However, to some extent this is balanced by the fact that nineteen of them, but very few in other groups, pointed out that the role was a marginal one between management and the girls which involved the steward in almost perpetual conflict. If we add together those who gave one or both responses we find that 39% of the full-time women mentioned the effect that becoming a shop-steward can have on the individual's personal relationships in the work situation. It seems they were concerned about such personal relationships but, in keeping with our earlier observations, they tended to see the role as one of helping rather than coming into conflict with the workers.

There is an obvious difference between the pattern of responses offered by the night men and the full-time women. This difference is made problematic by the fact that the night shift as a group professed the strongest commitment to the trade union organisation in the plant, and also seemed least likely to

Table 6.11 *Main disadvantages of being a shop-steward* *

Response	Day men		Night men		Full-time women		Part-time women	
	No.	%	No.	%	No.	%	No.	%
Bad relations with management	11	17	4	9	12	11	1	1
Bad relations with the workers	34	53	31	67	28	26	37	47
Marginal role which involves argument	3	5	1	2	19	17	3	4
Time	7	11	4	9	15	14	8	10
Other	6	9	1	2	6	6	8	10
Nothing	12	19	12	26	11	10	9	12
Don't know	2	3	3	7	32	29	23	29
Total	75	117	56	122	123	113	89	114

* Respondents were allowed two responses to this question, see table 3.2.

value the social relationships that they developed with their mates at work. Also, in the light of their instrumental orientation toward work it is surprising that so few of them mentioned the amount of leisure-time that the stewards were expected to devote to union activities.

For night men to be more likely than other groups to see the attractions of the steward's role in higher status rather than helping workmates is not surprising. What is surprising is the large proportion (almost as high as among the day men and far more than the women) who gave critical answers implying the stewards were out for themselves. Then there was high consensus in regarding the major drawback of the role as conflict between stewards and workers. Nor does it seem reasonable to dismiss this as a reason of low salience, on the grounds that they put little stress on social relationships, for we find that it was for just such reasons that virtually no-one was prepared to stand for office — whatever the status attractions might be. To keep things in perspective we should also note that just over a quarter of these men saw no disadvantages in being a shop-steward.

However we still need to explain the generally unsympathetic view that pervaded this shift, and contrasted so surprisingly with the attitudes of the full-time women.

To do this we need to go back to our earlier point that an organising campaign is liable to create conflicts within the workforce. The importance of this may be seen in the objective differences that existed between the union on the day and night shift and between the men and the women. The union was most strongly developed on the night shift, where strong pressure was brought to bear within the shop-stewards committee, by the senior stewards, in favour of developing a strong organisation with a consistent policy on the shift. The main issue during the period of interviewing was the level of membership in the plant, and particularly on the night shift. The senior stewards on the night shift intended to enforce a 'one hundred per cent union shop', and they frequently claimed that they were moving to a point where they could demand a 'show of cards' and enforce a refusal to work with all 'noners'. One of the main responsibilities of the steward in this situation was to work toward a 'full section'. We would argue that in these circumstances the potentialities for conflict between the steward and his membership are heightened, and that this is the main reason why the high level of interaction between night workers and their stewards entailed this appreciable element of tension.

The relations of the part-time women to the stewards were different again. In this group they were characterised by a certain remoteness. As a group they had least contact with stewards; most could not name their steward and of those who could, few saw him often. Only one was interested in the possibility of becoming a steward and large numbers were unable to answer the questions on the attractions and drawbacks of the role. Those who did answer tended not to show the full-time women's sympathetic perceptions. They saw the main disadvantage lying in conflict with workers (ignoring 'Don't knows' the frequency of this answer is similar to the night shift) while they mentioned 'interest' as often as 'helping the girls' among the attractions. To understand this remoteness and lack of sympathy it should be recalled that none of the stewards was drawn from this group.

JOINT CONSULTATION

Finally, we shall look at the attitudes of the workers toward the Joint Consultation and their relationship with that system. We remember, initially, that the management at Brompton had a strong traditional commitment to the consultative system and saw it as a more appropriate way of solving many problems than union-based bargaining.

Of those interviewed in the main sample, only one man on the day shift and one full-time woman were members of a Departmental or Works Committee. Two day men and one full-time woman had sat on a committee at some time in the past. It is interesting to note that this is in sharp contrast to the level of participation among shop-stewards. Of these stewards, seven day men and one night man were committee members, while a further two had stood unsuccessfully and would stand again in the future. One woman steward was a committee member and another was a past member.[23]

In table 6.12 we see that the majority of the non-members in all groups had never considered standing for a committee, and had no intention of standing in the future.

Table 6.12 *Future participation in the consultative committee*

	Day men	Night men	Full-time women	Part-time women	All
Not considered standing — not stand in future	55	44	99	74	272
Not considered standing — stand in future	5	2	5	–	12
Considered standing — stand in future	1	–	3	4	8
Total	61	46	107	78	292

Given this overwhelming lack of interest in standing for the position of representative, it will be of interest to look more closely at the relationship between the workers and the committee representatives, and to compare this with the earlier discussion of the trade union. Only a third of the men on day shift, just over half of the men on night shift, 43% of full-time women and no more than 10% of the part-time women were able to name their

---

23 This relationship between involvement in the trade union and joint consultative committees has been noted in other studies. E.g. see J. A. Banks, *Industrial Participation.* However, it may be dangerous to explain such patterns in terms of the personality of the union activist. In Brompton, domination of joint consultative committees — which they saw as a potential threat to their negotiating position — was the explicit policy of the shop-stewards. The stewards therefore were *expected* to stand for office by the senior stewards and the full-time official.

Departmental Committee or Works Committee Representative. Substantially more, it will be recalled, could name their union representative, even though many of the sample were not union members. The phenomenally low percentage of part-time women who were able to answer the question is further indication of their low involvement. Of those workers who were aware of the name of their representative, only a few were on extremely friendly terms with him or her. Most of the men saw themselves as being on quite friendly terms with their representatives, while large proportions of both groups of women said that they didn't really know their representative personally. Interaction with representatives, therefore, tended to be low.

Against this background it is interesting that a substantial proportion of those who knew the member did consult him on committee business; over half these men, three-quarters of the part-time women and 39% of full-time women had seen their representatives about the work of the committees. Out of the whole sample this represents 28% of the night men but appreciably less in the other groups, down to a mere 8% of part-time women. Furthermore, there were only two people, both night men, who claimed to see their committee member as often as once a month, compared with fifty-seven who saw their steward at least one a month.

Altogether, participation in the joint consultative committee system appeared to be very low. Few of the workers were interested in standing for the committees, and the rest rarely saw their representative on committee business. The part-time women have once more revealed their lower involvement by an almost total lack of interest in, and knowledge of, the committee system. On the other hand, the night shift again appeared to be slightly atypical, in that its members were more likely to know their representative and see him occasionally than were workers on the day shift. This is further testament to the less formal pattern of relationships on the night shift, which was facilitated by its small size and social isolation. More importantly, perhaps, it reflects the fact that the trade union organisation on the night shift tended to dominate the committee system to a greater extent than on the day shift. Most of the committee representatives on the night shift were, in fact, union shop-stewards. In general, however, we can say that the joint consultative committee system appeared to have made little impression upon the work situation of the labour force.

This point is developed in table 6.13, giving the responses when workers were questioned directly on the importance of the joint consultative committees.

Here we see that, except for the night men, a really substantial proportion were unable to comment on the importance of the committee system. Among

Table 6.13 *How important are the committees at Gourmets?*

	Day men	Night men	Full-time women	Part-time women	All No.	%
An absolute must	2	3	6	2	13	4
Very important	19	14	25	12	70	24
Quite important	8	13	17	12	50	17
Not really important	6	11	10	2	29	10
Not important at all	–	–	–	1	1	–
Don't know	29	5	51	49	134	45
Total	64	46	109	78	297	100

the night men there were 11% who could not answer, but the figure rises to 45% of the day men, 47% of the full-time women, and as many as 63% of the part-time women. Indeed, many of the part-time women were unaware of the existence of a committee system until they were interviewed. All this is, in itself, evidence that the committee system did not make much impact on the individual worker. However, only about 10% actually said that the committees were unimportant, though rather more of the night men.[24] Of those who felt competent to discuss the committees, the majority thought they had some importance, about half rating them as 'very important' or, occasionally, as 'an absolute must'.

It was immediately obvious, however, that responses to questions on the committee structure tended to be devoid of meaning. The committees were never criticised bitterly and neither were their praises sung by any respondent. The worker who was aware of the committees tended to be so in a vague uncommitted way. The respondents who thought the committees important invariably explained their responses in terms like 'they're a good thing', and on no occasion did a respondent become more explicit than that. Table 6.14 substantiates this point.

In sharp contrast to the responses on this question in the union section (table 6.6, page 125), a large proportion was unable to answer this question. The night shift were again atypical in that they were much more prone to give

---

24 Of those expressing definite opinions the percentages who said the committees were unimportant were: night men 27%, day men 17%, full-time women 14%, part-time women 10%.

Table 6.14 *How would you feel if the joint consultative committees were unable to continue at Gourmets?*

	Day men	Night men	Full-time women	Part-time women	All
Very badly	3.	7	5	3	18
Quite badly	14	9	9	10	42
Not really mind	16	12	23	4	55
Not mind at all	9	14	25	12	60
Don't know	22	4	47	49	122
Total	64	46	109	78	297

a positive response – only 9% of them were unable to answer compared with 34% of the day men, 43% of the full-time women and 63% of the part-time women.

Of those respondents who were able to comment, the typical response expressed no concern for the future of the committees. The number of responses declined progressively with increased concern. Altogether only 27% of the day men, 35% of the night men, 13% of the full-time women and 17% of the part-time women thought that they would miss the committees in any way.

From the above discussion it is clear that the joint committee structure at this factory had failed to make anything but a minor impact upon the worker. On the day shift, the majority of workers were generally ignorant of the committees and their functions, and were rarely involved in their operations. The night shift, because of its basic atypical feature, provided a situation in which the worker was much better informed about the committees, but in this situation he was just as likely, if not more likely, to dismiss them as irrelevant. The committees appeared to be fundamentally unable to exercise an identifiable influence over the work life of the worker, and so they were either ignored or thought to be essentially ineffective.

SUMMARY

In this chapter we have considered the various aspects of the system whereby the workers' interests *vis-à-vis* management were formally expressed. We have done this at some length because it is in this area of conflict and collective action that we can best see the expression of the orientations and attitudes discussed earlier. We have argued that to understand behaviour with respect to grievances and representation, it is not adequate to consider only the nature of the work and prior orientations. Just as perceptions of the work situation are mediated through prior orientations and actual experience of work, so perceptions of the system of representation depend on orientations and experience of that system – particularly the trade union – at work.

Subjective feelings of conflict in the work situation followed the expected pattern; day men and full-time women were appreciably more likely to feel they had a genuine cause for complaint. However the frequencies with which members of the groups did something about such grievances showed a different pattern.

The low commitment to work of the part-time women was again evident in their tendency to do nothing about their complaints. Indeed the most striking thing about this group was the large proportion who had no opinion on all aspects of representation. As a group they showed little interest in the union, though this was partly because no effort was made to encourage their interest.

In contrast the men of the night shift, who also had relatively few complaints, usually did something about them. They were also the group who were least critical of, and most involved in the union at Brompton. About three-quarters were members. Undoubtedly this is related to their higher involvement in work, but a comparison between the full-time women and men of the day shift saves us from too simple an explanation along these lines.

Both groups had frequent complaints but it was the women who tended to take them up while the men were scarcely more inclined to act than the part-time women. Nor could these two groups be easily characterised with regard to attitudes towards the union. In each there was a strong current of criticism of the local branch which, in the case of the men only, included criticism of the stewards, yet the men were much more likely to be union members. On the other hand the women, although mostly outside the union, generally followed a collective approach in handling complaints. To make sense of these differences we need to look more closely at the structure of worker representation in the factory.

The firm's traditional system of joint consultation was not very effective at Brompton. This is not to say that it did not do anything useful, but only one in five of the workers thought they would mind if it packed up. By contrast we see the importance for the workers of the trade union. Feelings were very much stronger on all matters relating to the union. This was partly due to the tendency for the union to dominate the worker side of the consultative committees, but it leaves no doubt as to what was seen as the significant form of worker representation.

Attitudes to trade unionism in general were predominantly favourable, the great majority of men and women expressing ideological support. However, there was much criticism of the local branch, and whether or not people were members bore little relationship to their attitudes to unionism in general or to the organisation at Brompton.

The union was in the process of trying to strengthen its organisation in the plant. It had been established in the factory from the start but had never been fully accepted, and less than half of the workers were members at the time of the study. The leadership, and so the impetus for greater unionisation, came from the men, particularly the night shift. However, the night shift was not disposed towards developing an organisation across the plant; in their attitude towards unionism they expressed the quintessence of their collective isolation from the workers on the day shift. The night shift's isolationist strategy caused complications for the leadership on the day shift, which was dominated by male operatives working on the process technology. These men, faced with a non-cooperative night shift and management's opposition to the development of the union, were also handicapped by their belief (shared with the night men) that the women could never be organised. Consequently their impact was not particularly successful. They had recruited two-thirds of the men and most of these were well disposed to the union, but there was also considerable criticism from both members and non-members, while for many of the women workers the shop-stewards were 'bosses' men'.

Ironically, the stewards' attempts to increase membership were hampered by the tensions their efforts created, and there were some bitter criticisms from among the men of both the day and night shifts. In spite of this, however, there was considerable solidarity among the night men; the union was generally seen as 'their' union, a going concern making the night man's job reasonable. This contrasts sharply with the position among the day men. Particularly striking was the low level of contact between these men and their stewards. Partly a result of the social isolation of the day men from each other and from the women, this lack of contact added to the isolation. The day men were generally dissatisfied with their work, looked to the union for support but felt that it failed them. Consequently they lapsed into frustrated inertia, seeing the union as part of the generally oppressive work environment.

The full-time women were equally, if not more dissatisfied with the union, but they were not under pressure to join and most of them were not members. Their criticism was of an organisation run by the men, and their antagonism to the local leadership did not apply to their own stewards. Here we see an interesting variant on the usual pattern where workers evaluate their union organisation in terms of the representatives with whom they came into contact. In this case the women stewards *belonged* to the group and were trying to fulfil the role of 'looking after the girls' which the supervisors had failed to fill. No recruiting campaign had stirred up internal hostilities and the solidarity of the women was essentially independent of the union.

In this chapter we have seen the consequences of the male stereotype of women as not interested in unionism. It is, therefore, a particularly interesting finding that far from being 'bad union material', the women workers at Brompton, particularly those who worked full-time, were potentially active union members. What is also obvious, however, is that the style of unionism adhered to by the women differed considerably from that of the men.

Finally, we have noted a generally favourable attitude towards the principle of trade-unionism, which may be seen as an element within a rudimentary working class consciousness. However, the effect of such consciousness upon the workers' support for a particular organisation depends on their experience of conflicts within the work situation. Those who thought that the existence of a strong trade union would be an important consideration in choosing a job were exceptions. But if trade unionism was not valued as part of a job, it was important as a means of securing satisfactory treatment in the job, and most criticisms of the union came from those who were most discontented in their work.

7 Conclusions

In the preceding chapters we have examined the worker's involvement in their employment situation, looking in turn at their perceptions of the firm, their jobs, supervision and representation. Our analysis has revealed an appreciable amount of dissatisfaction among the workers. It is, therefore, important to recall that this cannot be attributed to an unusually bad situation. It is true the intrinsic nature of the work was not attractive, but it was no worse than a great many other industrial jobs. Apart from this, Gourmets is the sort of firm which would generally be regarded as a good employer. Indeed, at a superficial level the workers were quite satisfied with their jobs at Gourmets. The discontent arose from the sort of factors which are widely experienced by manual workers in our society. A detailed consideration of alienation and social class is obviously beyond the scope of this study. We have been mainly concerned to describe variations in the way different groups of workers perceive their class position. However, this emphasis should not conceal the facts of class inequality or that very few of the workers at Brompton derived any pleasure from the work they performed.

Nevertheless, it is important to recognise that quite significant patterns of differentiation exist within the working class as a whole, and also within the labour force of a particular factory. One of the attractions of the Brompton factory for us was the opportunity it afforded to examine comparatively the patterns of involvement of women and men of different ages and family circumstances.

Women form a large and extremely important segment of the working class. Some 37% of the national labour force are women, and over half of them are married; they are paid much less than men and only a quarter of them are members of a trade union.[1] It is unfortunate, therefore, that industrial sociologists have paid such little attention to women workers. True, there have been studies of women but these have, in the main, been either human relations experiments or studies concerned with the particular problems created by 'women's two roles'.[2] 'Women' have almost become a

---

1 See *Social Trends*, No. 1 and Audrey Hunt, *A Survey of Women's Employment.*
2 For a review of the human relations literature and the role that women workers have played in a number of the most significant experiments see P. Blumberg, *Industrial Democracy* and L. Baritz, *The Servants of Power.*

separate subject area. Composite pictures of manual workers, and studies of the working class invariably deal solely with men. Where sociologists have attempted to compare the attitudes of men and women workers they have tended to present descriptive generalisations, without theoretical content, raising questions such as whether women are more satisfied than men. Not surprisingly, different studies get unexplainable contradictory results.[3] Such a question posed with our data would also give contradictory results, but our interest is in explaining how different levels of satisfaction arise, rather than looking for correlations with a single variable, whether sex or anything else.

A general explanation of the way work is experienced must take account of the objective features of the particular work situation and the whole range of social characteristics of the workers in that situation. In other words, experience within the social structure of the work situation must be related to the individual's position within the social structure of the wider society.

LIVING WITH WORK

The workers in the Brompton factory were all in the same labour market in the geographical sense; that is they wanted employment in the same area and hence from the same employers. To a large extent the types of work available to them fell within the same skill range and they were doing similar jobs. However, they did not share a common market situation in the sense of being in competition for the same jobs. Night-shift work, at higher pay, was limited to men over the age of 21 — though all men could choose day-shift work; on days the firm operated a distinction between men's and women's work, which was reinforced by the attitudes of the workers and accompanied by a typical sex difference in rates of pay. Among the women there was the further distinction between those wanting part-time and those wanting full-time employment. As we have seen, these differences in market situation were reflected in other important differences in the workforce.

There exists quite an extensive literature on the problems women face in taking a job. See, for example, V. Klein, *Britain's Married Women Workers*; I.L.O., *Women Workers in a Changing World*; P. Jephcott *et al., Married Women Working*. Few studies, however, have looked at the distinctive features of women in the work situation. The studies by Lupton, *On the Shop Floor*, and Cunnison, *Wages and Work Allocations*, are exceptional in this respect.

3 See C. L. Hulin and P. C. Smith, 'Sex Differences in Job Satisfaction'. After reviewing other studies and noting the contradictory findings, they seek to settle the matter with their own study. As there is no theoretical underpinning they merely produce another addition to the list of findings on one side of this pointless dispute.

These market differences relate to the particular firm studied, but to a large extent they are relevant to the whole labour market. For instance the distinction between men's work and women's work applies to pretty well all manual work, and indeed, to most other areas of employment.

It is, however, an important point that our sample consists of workers who had all chosen the same employer. In so far as they were responding to the general image of the firm it could be argued that they were making the same choice, though our evidence shows they perceived this choice in different ways and not in terms of a common stereotype. They worked in the same environment, subject to the same management, and with the same conditions of service, including systems of payment and fringe benefits, social facilities and so on. Also there was only one union to represent them and a system of joint consultation which applied to the whole factory. But all these aspects of their common situation could impinge differently on individuals or groups of workers. Other aspects of their employment situation were more general in their relevance. The market situation of the firm itself was a common factor for all employees, *vis-à-vis* other firms, though its effect within the firm was mediated through personnel policies. On the other hand the social identity and status within the community, derived from working for a large well-known employer, varied only with the worker's social contacts outside work.

Given these basic similarities in the workers' employment situation, we nevertheless found considerable variation in the ways in which different workers had come to understand the work situation and their position in it. We were able to relate these variations to the four main groups we have identified. The groups tended to have significantly different perceptions of work, arising, in large measure, from differences in non-work social characteristics, particularly their positions within the family.

The demands made upon women by marriage and childbirth in our society have meant that women in general have tended to develop a much lower commitment to employment than have men. This tendency for women to centre their lives around their position in the home has been reinforced by severe discrimination against them in the employment market. Perhaps the most glaring example of this pattern of reinforcement in recent years was provided by the *News of the World* in its exposure of the incredibly low wages paid by Conway Stewart, the pen company, to married women who assembled pens in their homes. Most of these women regarded pen-assembly as a hobby and in no way considered that they had grounds for complaint.[4]

---

4 *News of the World*, 20 and 27 April 1969.

As a group, working-class women form the most highly exploited section of the labour force. Given this, it is not surprising that many women regard being a housewife and bringing up a family as more important and rewarding than the meaningless, alienating jobs that are available to them. Increasingly, however, married women are working. This is because of economic pressures but also because life at home, when the family are growing up and the children are out at school, can be extremely lonely. Nevertheless, they still attach low importance to work, which in their eyes may not be 'real work'. This tendency was noticeable in Brompton. Many of the married women who were employed part-time did not regard themselves as 'real workers'. As such they could be strongly sympathetic toward trade unionism without ever contemplating taking out a union card.

The part-time shift comprised married women with children. In some cases the children had grown up and started work (making it easier for the mother to have a job) but most of the women had children who were still dependent. Their reasons for working were typically a combination of economic and social considerations, viewed from a distinctive, married women's perspective. Their economic interest was to some extent based on fundamental necessity but even here the problems of job security and the actual level of income were less important for the women than for their husbands. They worked to supplement the family income but within the range open to them the actual amount was not so important. The other main reason for working was escape from the loneliness at home to the companionship of work. Once friendships were established at work there was, therefore, a reluctance to change jobs to maximise earnings.

Normally in our society it is only married women who have a real choice of whether to work or not. It has become quite usual for women to carry on at work after marriage, but the question of stopping work then arises with motherhood. Once out of employment the question is not only whether to start again but also when and for how long. A return to employment may be felt to be only temporary, hence the low concern with job security and the high labour turnover among part-time women.

Under these circumstances the significant economic question is whether there is the extra income at all, while the precise level is of very secondary importance. At the same time the actual social rewards are almost impossible to judge before entering employment. Therefore, in terms of the main reasons for working, the fundamental decision is whether to work. The question of where to work then arises in terms of finding employment, because it is not always easy for a mother to find somewhere suitable.

The main problem is that most jobs entail working at times when mothers want to be at home to look after their families.[5] As a result the commonest type of employment for married working class women is part-time cleaning. Before joining Gourmets several of the women in our part-time sample had done this while many of the others had done equally low-paid jobs in school canteens or local shops. Most often of all, however, they had been at home. Part-time factory work is still relatively unusual, and working at Gourmets was the first experience of it for these women. Gourmets themselves had radically changed their policy over the years. In the good old paternalistic days at Longborough they gave a girl a wedding present of a Bible and the sack; now at both Longborough and Brompton they needed the services of married women and had adapted to this, even to the extent of running special part-time shifts. This was very important from the workers' point of view. It can hardly be said that they found factory work attractive but the firm was easy to get to and, above all, the hours could be conveniently fitted in with their family commitments. This was the basis of their understanding of work at Gourmets.

This group of women had low commitment to work which was, for them, very much secondary to being a wife and mother. They were glad of the opportunity to fit in a few hours in a job, providing extra money and company. Beyond this their expectations were very low. Consequently they were well disposed to the firm and relatively uncritical of their experience at work. Altogether they had the lowest expectations and those they considered important were most adequately met, so they were the most satisfied of all the workers.[6]

There were also married women working full-time, though many of them were younger than the part-time women and as yet had no children. A minority were in similar family positions to the part-time workers but showed

5 The proportion of women doing part-time work seems to have been on the increase during the 1960s (9% of all women over age 15 in 1961 and 13% in 1966). See *Social Trends*, No. 1, p. 68. Nevertheless, as a group they were in a much worse position even than women who were able to work full-time. Some 19% of all part-time women workers were employed as unskilled manual workers, as compared with only 2% of full-time workers. See A. Hunt, *A Survey of Women's Employment*, vol. II, p. 20. In the Soviet Union, the employment of married women is assisted by the provision of supervised activities for children while they are not in school during working hours. Even this is far from adequate. See N. T. Dodge, *Women in the Soviet Economy.*

6 It is not surprising, in view of what we have said, that this group also had the highest labour turnover. However, turnover has often been used as an indicator of low satisfaction. This shows the danger of using a behavioural indicator without paying attention to its theoretical basis.

greater commitment to employment or greater economic need by choosing to work full-time. Typically, however, the full-time women were at an earlier stage in the life-cycle than those on the part-time shifts. They were young and single or fairly recently married and without children. They had worked continuously since leaving school — indeed a number were in their first jobs, but they could expect to leave work to raise a family in the future. In addition there were several older, single women, and childless married women who had always worked and were likely to continue to do so in future. However, few had the responsibilities which men can expect to encounter at some stage in their lives.

Most of the women who worked full-time did have to support themselves, however, so good pay and security were quite important to them. As we might expect, their interest in security lay between that of the part-time women and that of the men. Pay is a basic expectation from any employment and their personal circumstances could lead to them putting some emphasis on this reward, but in general their expectations were not particularly high. As Gourmet's offered women relatively high pay and a secure job anyway, these women tended to be satisfied with their position on these counts. It was their experience when at work which gave rise to considerable discontent.

They had little experience of factory jobs, and did not much care for the type of work they had to do. Many of them found the work boring and tedious. However, they did not have high expectations of the intrinsic job so this was not a major cause of dissatisfaction. Where they did expect some satisfaction from their work was in social relationships, and it was here that they were critical of the firm. They claimed a high level of grievances, with discontent focused on the control system — on the organisation of work, the rules and above all the supervision. Their expectations were higher than those of the part-time group while their treatment was generally less good — management had no reason to make the same effort to accommodate them with regard to family needs and supervisors treated the youngsters with less respect than the older, married women of the part-time group. Consequently they were less satisfied.

Their main attachment to their jobs lay in friendships with workmates. Not only was this the chief source of social reward, but not having the family responsibilities of the part-time women, they were more likely to develop close friendships — even with supervisors. The closeness of their relations with fellow workers may be seen in their collective approach to the handling of grievances. The level of demands they made of their jobs and this collective orientation would have made them good union material if the men running the union had been able to recognise their potential. As it was, the union took little interest in their problems and the women saw it as part of the hostile control system. At the same time they had a particularly favourable view of their stewards, whom they saw as their own representatives rather than agents of the union.

Most of the women who worked full-time at Brompton had family circumstances which were unlikely to lead to a strong instrumental commitment to work, or to a high level of family centredness. Together with the fact that they worked a full day, this led them, almost by default, to have greater expectations from their time at work. They neither wanted or expected to 'get on' and the money was quite good. What they did want was a pleasant time whilst they were at work, and this was often prevented by the firm through its supervision and its general organisation of production. Any pleasure to be got from working at Brompton was created by the girls themselves. Not unnaturally the satisfaction they gained from each other's company did not, in general, lead them to a more favourable assessment of the firm.

The group which contrasted most clearly with the women were the men on the night shift. Like the part-time women they tended to be family centred and interested in hours of work which gave them time with their families, but there the similarity ends. A man's occupation is a source of social identity and determines the style of life for him and his family. Consequently his commitment to work is normally high, regardless of how much enjoyment he derives from it. Among the night men the commitment was distinctly instrumental.

Family responsibilities, coupled in many cases with experience of unemployment, led them to put a high value on job security. In their jobs at Gourmets they felt they were as secure as they could hope to be. Pay was also important and by working nights they gained an extra premium of almost 20%. However, this did not lead to the same level of satisfaction as in the case of security. Almost all thought the pay was fairly reasonable but only half actually described it as good. Their wages were not particularly high but probably they were as good or better than these men were likely to get elsewhere in the area. This was recognised by the men who were, therefore, quite glad to have their current jobs, though they couldn't really enthuse about the level of earnings. For the older workers, present wages tended to matter less than future income after retirement, so the firm's pension scheme was appreciated by them, and other fringe benefits such as the sick pay scheme were generally appreciated by the night men.

In addition to these economic considerations they also valued the good working conditions. In general, though, they put relatively little emphasis on rewards related to the work itself. The informal pattern of relationships on

150

the night shift meant that they did not share the day shift's sense of an oppressive control system. No doubt this helped to reduce concern with the rewards of the actual work situation, but they did not maximise the associated opportunities for social rewards. Like the part-time women they tended not to make close friends but unlike the women they didn't particularly feel the need for companionship either. Social relations provided a weak basis for attachment to the job, and the actual job content an even weaker one. They would gladly change to more interesting work, if they thought they could get it, but this was not of prime importance. Their satisfaction on more salient rewards made them less disposed to leave Gourmets. With the part-time women they showed more favourable attitudes to the firm than the other two groups.

In short the night men tended to be family centred with primarily instrumental orientations, and as their main expectations were fairly well met they had a favourable perception of their employment. Their perceptions were somewhat less favourable than those of the part-time women, which is not surprising in view of their higher expectations, but on the whole they were rather more favourable than those of the full-time women. Nevertheless, one hesitates to say they were positively satisfied. They saw work as a necessity from which they could not hope to get much satisfaction. Their work at Gourmets was as deadly as it comes, but they had a good steady job with a reasonable firm, and that's what mattered. But even this was not to be had without a struggle; the union was necessary to gain and maintain this position. At the individual level grievances were not particularly frequent, but when they arose they were usually taken up.

By far the most discontented group were the day men. Although some of them had the most interesting jobs in the factory, these still fell short of expectations. In other respects, also, they felt dissatisfied with the level of rewards. It would be a mistake to think of these men as greatly dissatisfied with every aspect of their employment; under such circumstances they would have been unlikely to stay with Gourmets. Nevertheless the sum total of their discontent was quite impressive.

To some extent their evaluations were the result of high expectations. This is particularly relevant to comparisons with the women. In relation to the night shift the position is less clear. Both groups of men had high commitment to work in general, though from somewhat different standpoints, with the older, night men perhaps having a slightly higher commitment. On the other hand the day men had more utopian expectations; they were more aware of the possibilities of what work might be like and the gap between this and their actual experience.

The day men tended to be young and single, or if married to have less children than the night men. Thus many of them lacked the economic incentive of family responsibilities, and so were less able to obtain instrumental satisfaction from work. To be sure they regarded pay and security as important and they were not badly off in these respects, but their economic needs were not as specific, or their rewards as great, as those of the men on the night shift. As with the full-time women, the absence of family responsibilities led indirectly to greater expectations from the time spent at work, and in this case also to a desire to 'get on'. But here the rewards were disappointing. The promotion system was felt to be very unsatisfactory and (again like the full-time women) the control system was a source of tension. The young men were particularly irked by the supervision on days, which we may contrast with the informal relations of the night shift. They would have liked to feel their jobs were worthwhile but could not see them this way. All in all they were the group who were least likely to feel that the aspects of work they regarded as important were the best catered for, or that they were well catered for. Consequently their job satisfaction and attachment to the firm were the lowest of all groups.

In analysing patterns of involvement in work, it may be helpful to think of three levels of generality. The broadest relates to the labour market, being involvement in work in general. Here the main reward is security and the main division of workers is between male and female, because of their non-work social roles. The second level is the firm, where extrinsic rewards are particularly (though not exclusively) relevant, and attachment may be highly fickle in so far as it is based on instrumental orientations. The main division at this level, arising from family roles, was between married and single workers, the married having more favourable perceptions. Thirdly there is the level of the actual work experience in the job, entailing the intrinsic job, the control system and inter-personal relations. Here there was no clear division, the groups having different evaluations of various aspects but in general this level was a source of discontent concerning the job and the control system, though relations with other workers provided some compensation, especially for the women.

We have seen that among both the men and the women the younger workers were generally less satisfied. Such an inverse relation between age and satisfaction has been noted often,[7] and it might be argued that this is, in itself, the explanation of the differences we have observed. To some extent we think it probable that such an explanation is relevant. It does seem that the young workers' higher, more utopian expectations were beaten

---

7 See, for example, A. Kornhauser, *Mental Health of the Industrial Worker.*

down by experience to a sort of resignation where a number of hours at work were tolerated for the extrinsic rewards. However, this alone is far too simple an explanation. Far more than this happens to the pattern of life as the worker grows older; it is not age itself which is relevant but the social experience it reflects. We have attempted to show some of the ways such experience influences perceptions of work.

SOME IMPLICATIONS FOR THE STUDY OF WORK

In the first chapter of this paper we drew attention to the schools of thought which have dominated the sociological study of work and workplace behaviour. While our main concern here has been to offer a descriptive account of work in a particular factory, our study does raise several points of relevance to the sort of explanations that have been offered by industrial sociologists. In particular the evidence we have presented has an important bearing upon the recent debate that has taken place between sociologists of the 'technological implications' school and those who have attempted to develop an 'action approach' in the study of work.

Technology

Technology has come to be regarded by many industrial sociologists as the important determinant of workplace behaviour. It has been widely argued that job satisfaction is dependent on production technology, with conveyor belt mass production work being least satisfying, in contrast to jobs in craft or process technology.[8] Satisfying work has also been seen as positively related to integration in the work group and identification with the firm. Thus Woodward has argued that 'moves into the continuous process area of production facilitated *almost automatically* the building up of harmonious and contributive human relationships'.[9] Group integration has, furthermore, been related to forms of collective action. Thus Sayles[10] has classified the behaviour of work groups into four main categories — apathetic, erratic, strategic and conservative — and related them to the type of technology. In this scheme, mass production technology promotes apathetic or erratic behaviour from workers while process technology is more likely to foster strategic behaviour.

While none of the authors who stress the influence of technology entirely ignores the subjective desires and wants of the workers, it is fair to say that

---

8 See, for example, R. Blauner, *Alienation and Freedom.*
9 J. Woodward, 'Automation and Technical Change: The Implication for the Management Process'. (Our emphasis.)
10 L. R. Sayles, *The Behaviour of Industrial Work Groups.*

their overwhelming tendency has been to relegate this subjectivity to a subordinate role. For them the attitudes and behaviour of workers tend to be seen as a direct, one-to-one reflection of the technological structure of the workplace.

At this point it will be useful to refer to the details of the Brompton situation. Most of the jobs in the Brompton factory related to mass production processes and involved conveyor belt packaging work. Among the women and the night-shift men the main job was working directly on the belt, with a handful in the more responsible role of wrapping machine operator. In addition there were a substantial number of auxiliaries servicing for the belt workers. These auxiliary jobs gave the workers greater freedom of movement but it is doubtful if they felt much less tied to the machines; we noted that they were more likely than the women directly on the belts to feel the pace of work was too much for them. The night-shift men had rather less auxiliaries and the part-time women less machine operators. Apart from these there were several time workers in each of the groups who were either non-manual, with relatively high status, or manual with relatively low status compared with the rest of the workforce. The real contrast, however, is with the men of the day shift who were either process operatives or belt auxiliaries doing work which gave them far greater autonomy than their female counterparts.

The arguments of theorists in the 'technological implications' school would clearly lead us to predict a considerably greater degree of job satisfaction (or lack of dissatisfaction) among the men on the day shift and among the timeworkers of all shifts; these were the workers who were free of the mass-production technology. Bearing in mind that the night men were doing 'women's work' and that more than any other group they were in a position to look back on more agreeable jobs, we would expect these men to experience the greatest dissatisfaction.

In fact the result was not so straightforward. Looking only at attitudes to the job itself, the time workers do emerge as the most satisfied, especially the non-manual workers, such as inspectors, with potentially more interesting work. Most of those who gained any real intrinsic job satisfaction were in this category. Apart from these workers, there was a general high level of discontent with the nature of the work; most found it frustrating and monotonous while few gained any sense of achievement, apart from some of the women who 'felt good' when they completed their quota. Again in line with our 'technological' prediction, the night shift workers were most critical of the lack of interest in their work. However, this is as far as the prediction is borne out. The day men were almost as critical as the night shift and were actually the group most likely to find their jobs frustrating, while the women were generally more likely to find some interest in their work. Looking at attitudes in a wider context, overall satisfaction with employment bore no apparent relationship to the content of the work performed. The day men were not the most but the least satisfied group, while the night workers were second to the part-time women in being satisfied with their situation.[11]

To understand these findings we must first take account of the different ways in which the groups evaluated their jobs. The group of men on days, who were younger with less experience of work, tended to be more utopian in their evaluation; they judged their jobs in terms of what work might be like — in terms of jobs which they could conceive of themselves doing but in practice were never likely to have. In contrast the older, night-shift men saw their work from the standpoint of a resigned instrumentalism; they were conscious of economic coercion to take basically unrewarding work, and having made this adjustment they were a little less frustrated than the day men. The part-time women were least antagonistic to the work because they only had to stick if for four hours a day. But both groups of women also found little intrinsically attractive in their jobs, and those who did express satisfaction usually did so for rather slight reasons. However, this reveals the basis of their different evaluations; they had lower expectations of intrinsically rewarding work, evaluating their jobs more from a social standpoint in terms of relations with fellow workers, supervisors and union representatives.

The different evaluations are clearly based on the workers' orientations to work. When we look further at these orientations we find that no-one put a particularly high priority on the interest of the work. The day men probably had the highest expectations in this respect and so were dissatisfied even though their work was less deadly than that of the other groups. Overall perceptions, however, were mainly determined by factors other than the actual job content.

Workers within the same technological system, therefore, had quite different perceptions of that situation. Their behaviour also varied. Using Sayles' typology we would have expected erratic or apathetic behaviour from the packers on both the day and the night shifts. Such expectations were certainly destroyed by the behaviour of the men on the night shift.

---

11 The fact that technology was seen to have only a limited effect may be due, to some extent, to the limited range of the technological variable as compared with other relevant variables in the situation. Undoubtedly, also, the technology influenced the overall organisation of the plant and this would have an effect upon all the workers. It is impossible, however, to estimate the effect of this within a single case study.

These men had organised themselves through their trade union branch which they used in a decidedly strategic way. This organisation had an important impact upon the social structure of both the night shift and the whole Brompton factory. No-one who has seen a packing line in operation can doubt that its profitable operation sets limits upon the actions of any packer. However, to commit the packer's behaviour to the limbo of non-strategic aimlessness stretches the case a bit far. A packing line is not reducible to its technology. The worker relates to the belt through a particular structure of social relationships in the work situation. The technology is mediated through the culture of the work force and through a series of formal rules, neither of which is deducible directly from the technology of mass production. To argue, therefore, that sustained collective action is unlikely to emerge in work situations dominated by conveyor belts is to argue a one-sided case which ignores the influence of these other factors. In their strike action over the employment of students, and their general approach to grievances the night men at Brompton demonstrated that strategic action is possible in work situations that are dominated by mass production technology.

We have argued, therefore, that technology does have an important influence upon the attitudes and behaviour of industrial workers, but it is not their sole, or necessarily their main source. Technology is but one aspect of the employment situation, where all aspects may be experienced as rewards or deprivations. The way a worker perceives and responds to any particular mix in the various aspects of work depends on the orientations he brings into that situation.

Orientations

At this point it will be useful to outline the role that we consider 'orientations to work' should play within sociological analysis of the workplace. Throughout this paper we have made considerable use of this notion of actors' orientations toward the work situation, which we have posited to be a central organising principle whereby people make some sense of their lives. Our use of the notion was informed by the belief that people's ideas about work, and how work fits into their lives, are themselves important sources of variation in the attitudes and behaviour of industrial workers.

Against this it may be objected that only work factors have any influence on perceptions of work, while orientations are irrelevant. This would be the case if orientations, however measured, had no effect on reactions to the work situation, or if orientations arose entirely from the immediate work situation and so were redundant as explanatory variables. A rather milder objection would be that orientations may be relevant to workers' attitudes at the individual level but are randomly spread through the labour force

156

and so of no sociological interest. This would entail orientations playing no part in job selection, or otherwise there would be grouping of workers with similar orientations.

We suggest that the evidence we have presented shows both these theoretical positions to be untenable. We have argued that non-work factors are important in a number of ways. Through orientations they affect the way workers relate to their work situations, and also influence their choice of jobs, leading in Brompton to the formation of our four major groups, each with its distinctive pattern of non-work social characteristics, orientations and attitudes.

The tendency to express explanations in terms of work factors alone, to be found in much industrial sociology, is probably due to the apparent homogeneity of actors in responding to certain aspects of work. Thus, although some work factors, such as responsibility, may be an attraction or disadvantage, others such as pay or interesting work are normally desired by all. The better the pay or the more interesting the work, the better people are pleased. However, orientations do not merely refer to what is wanted but also to the salience of the wants. Thus interesting work may be the first priority and pay of relatively little importance or it might be the reverse. It is not sufficient to look at any reward in isolation since the worker's evaluation of any situation will depend on the levels of all rewards in relation to his priorities.

To argue for the use of 'orientations', however, is not to deny the importance of work-specific factors such as production technology and the like. In fact we found evidence of the effects of such variables, in the direction predicted, on the basis of existing theories. Although the observed effects were less marked than the influence of worker orientations we should resist the temptation to draw conclusions about relative importance. The basic theoretical point here is that involvement depends on the relationship between orientations and the objective features of the work situation. Which features are important in any concrete situation depends on the complex of expectations brought to that situation and how far these are met by the actual rewards received from work. Thus, to ask whether work factors or orientations are more important involves an inappropriate comparison; while to compare the influence of different factors in the abstract without reference to orientations is pointless and misleading.

The way in which work is experienced, therefore, depends neither on work factors nor orientations alone but on the interaction of the two. Just as the technological implications approaches to the study of workplace behaviour have tended to over-emphasise the influence of the work situation it would seem that recent attempts at an 'action approach' in British industrial sociology have come dangerously near to being stuck the other side of the factory gates. There is a danger that the importance of extra-work influences upon orientations and the independence of orientations in determining workplace attitudes and behaviour will be overstated. Thus, in their study of affluent workers in Luton, Goldthorpe and his colleagues, although well aware of the crucial relationship between orientations and work variables, seem too ready to explain the dominant attitudes of some workers on the basis of instrumental orientations which are created outside the factory and are largely unaffected by the worker's experiences within the factory. They argue, for example, that in considering their 'privatised' workers 'it would be a mistake here to think only, or even primarily, in terms of a process of individual adaptation to the conditions of the work situation objectively considered . . . the narrowing down of work expectations must be regarded not as a product of their in-plant socialisation, but rather of a prior orientation to work, on their part, of a decisively instrumental kind'.[12] While it is common for the empirical tradition within sociology to draw quite a clear distinction between 'work' and 'non-work' as areas of activity, the position is not so clear cut. It seems more reasonable to argue that the understanding which workers have of, and the meaning they give to work is derived from whole sets of *interrelated* experiences in the past, many of which will have been within work situations. For example, this means, at the very least, that workers who take a job on the night shift in a food factory, because they want the money and feel prepared to endure a boring job in order to get it, also take into that work situation definitions of 'shop-stewards' and 'managers' that they have developed through interaction with shop-stewards and managers in the past.

It can be argued that the tendency to overlook the significance of workplace experience is reinforced by the practice of classifying orientations into types on the basis of their dominant aspects, in as much as this leads to the neglect of an analysis of variation and experience on other aspects. While it would seem likely that workers' relationships with aspects of their work are patterned in some way,[13] to give a too severe primacy to such a simple notion as an 'instrumental orientation' is not justifiable.

There may well be prior instrumental orientations, although to some extent the orientations may be a result of adjustment to a situation of limited non-economic rewards. In either case, however, 'instrumental' only refers to the dominant character of these orientations and not the totality.

---

12 J. H. Goldthorpe *et al.*, *The Affluent Worker in the Class Structure*, pp. 67-8.
13 We should, however, be wary of attributing a consistency to these ideas, from the outside. See, for example, E. Gellner, 'Concepts and Society'.

For example, the evidence presented by Goldthorpe and his colleagues shows there was considerable dissatisfaction with the desire for improvement of non-economic rewards.[14] In so far as these workers were 'satisfied' it could be argued that it was because they had learnt to expect no more from work. The evidence of the Brompton factory would support such an interpretation. If, for example, we compare the full-time women with their male counterparts on the day shift we find that they had much lower expectations of an interesting job. They were decidedly less committed to work and an understanding of this lack of commitment obviously needs to take account of the position that women occupy within the family in our society. In a sense this may be seen as prior to their experience at Gourmets. However, it would be a mistake to infer from this that these women did not experience deprivations while at work. It would be an even greater mistake if our evidence were used to bolster the myth that 'women don't mind doing boring work' or, as we have often heard it, 'women prefer boring work'. No women mentioned the nature of the work as a major reason behind their choice of Gourmets. Quite the opposite in fact. The attraction of Gourmets, and of all factory work, for them is best seen as a repulsion from alternative forms of employment in shops and offices. While at work, most of them took the realistic view that all the jobs open to them were essentially the same and that friendship was all that they could expect to obtain from their hours in the factory. It was their position within the labour market in combination with their position within the family which produced their particular and distinctive orientation toward the workplace.

Given this, it seems clear that the ordering of particular orientations by work experience is an important area of study. The structure of the work situation should not be thrown out with the bathwater of technological determinacy and the like. Without this there is a danger that the existence of pre-established orientations will be over-emphasised, producing an alternative, yet equally static industrial sociology. In the Luton study, for example, it seems that orientations are attributed with a permanence that remains unaffected by experience of work. Whatever the particular features of the Luton situation, it would be unwise to introduce *a priori* into other studies similar assumptions about the relationship of orientations to work experience. Certainly on the evidence of the night-shift workers at Brompton it would seem that the relationship between dominantly instrumental orientations and workplace behaviour is far from being straightforward.

---

14 See J. H. Goldthorpe *et al.*, *The Affluent Worker: Industrial Attitudes and Behaviour*, chapter 3.

One of the requirements of an adequate sociological explanation should be that it considers the derivation of particular 'definitions of the situation' and examines the process whereby these are rejected, sustained or enforced. While it must be recognised that workers bring ideas and expectations into work situations it would be foolhardy to ignore the fact that while they are at work these ideas and expectations have to be related to the ideas and actions of other workers, as well as those of supervision and management. Ideally a study of a work situation should examine these processes. The neglect of management and supervision in the present study is one of its severest inadequacies. However, by looking at four distinct groups of workers, it does go some way toward an analysis which understands 'orientations' to be on-going processes affecting, and affected by action within particular concrete situations.

Groups and variables

Throughout, our argument has been built around the four main groups, yet much of the discussion has been based on variables, such as family responsibility, job or previous unemployment. Our groups were not homogeneous on important variables except for sex and, for the part-time group only, marital status. Thus, it could be argued that it would have been more appropriate to proceed in terms of variables. Undoubtedly there would be advantages in such an approach. At a simple level it would help with problems such as the treatment of the manual and non-manual timeworkers, who tended to be atypical of their groups but were not numerous enough to be regarded as further groups. At a more sophisticated level the use of a multivariate approach would help to push further the analysis of factors we have found to be relevant.

These considerations should not let us lose sight of the significant advantages to be gained from our analysis in terms of groups. In the first place it helps us to see the relevance of job choice. If workers have prior orientations we would expect them to select jobs accordingly, within the constraints of available choice. Such choice must take place at the general level, as covered by our groups, since workers have neither the knowledge nor opportunity for more precise selection.[15] Therefore, to the extent that there is a process of self-selection, the groups will comprise workers with similar orientations. It is true that if work factors were the sole cause of attitudes we would get the same observed results, but if orientations arise

---

15 To be precise, some workers can make more detailed choices, e.g. older workers seeking non-production time-work, while all can 'choose' by leaving jobs. However, it seems probable that selection operates primarily at the group level.

from non-work factors we will find the groups tend to be composed of workers with different social characteristics, and this we do find. If we treat social characteristics as background variables we will find them spread between groups, since selection processes will never produce perfectly homogeneous groups on all variables. Perceptions, however, depend on the interaction between orientations and objective rewards, so they will vary between groups for similar background variables.

The rewards gained from work are not all controlled by management. Part of the objective situation in which orientations are translated into attitudes is created by the workers themselves. Within the structural limits imposed by management, the workers create the patterns of social relationship, the degree of collective solidarity and friendliness. These are located within, and specific to groups of workers.

Finally there is the socialisation process within the group, which tends to produce common attitudes. Not all members of the group make the same evaluation on any one point, but there is a tendency towards agreement. Thus we found it was not always the same individuals who gave the dominant type of answers, though variation within groups tended to follow background variables.[16]

Each group provided a different social environment in which work was interpreted. If we consider the married men, for example, we see that those on the day shift, alongside young, single men and women, were in a quite different social environment from those on nights. On this basis alone it is not surprising that they tended to make different evaluations.

We would claim, in the light of these considerations, that our groups are valid social units, for which the patterns of perceptions may be taken, to some extent, as group properties. In the ideal situation our uses of groups and variables would have merged into an approach which treated groups themselves as variables. But, as always, there were practical and methodological obstacles to attaining the ideal. Further research may overcome some of the limitations of the present study and develop further the theoretical ideas discussed here. In the meantime we hope to have shed some light on an important subject. Our approach has, we believe, been a fruitful one which has served to raise a number of important issues. Work occupies a substantial part of peoples lives, its influence embraces their whole lives, and its meaning to the workers must be seen in this context. From this standpoint we have sought to add something to the understanding of the meaning of work.

---

16 Since our argument has been couched in terms of groups and variables it has been necessary throughout the analysis to take care to avoid the ecological fallacy.

Appendix: The interview schedule[1]

Department: Name:
Shift: Address:
Sex: Date of birth:
Code number:

SECTION 1. ATTITUDE TOWARD AND CONCEPTION OF THE FIRM
In this section I would like to ask you a few questions on how you, as a worker, think of Gourmets, and on how you think Gourmets compares with other firms.
1. How long have you been at Gourmets?
2. Why did you decide to come to Gourmets?
3. Had you worked for any other firm before?
   Dates   Job   Firm
4. Of all the firms that you have heard about or had experience of, how would you rate Gourmets?
   Show Card 1[2]
5. What do you like best about Gourmets?
6. What do you like least about Gourmets?
7. Do you think that being in a family firm makes a difference?
8. If you could change anything in Gourmets, what do you think it would be?

SECTION 2
I should now like to get some background information on your job situation; that is, the work you do, and the people that you have contact with while you are working.
9. What is your present job? (Probe here to find the social situation and responsibility of the job, together with the respondents actual knowledge of the process involved.)
10. How long have you been in this job?

---

1 This is the schedule used for the main sample. As indicated in chapter 1, shop-stewards were excluded from the main sample. They were asked substantially the same questions, except for those relating to participation in the union, but their responses have not been used directly in this study.
2 The cards are listed at the end of the schedule.

11. On the card are a list of things that people often have in mind when thinking about a job. Which of these would you say was the most important thing in a job for you?
    Show Card 2
12. Which would you say was the least important?
13. Now I would like you to grade each of these things in order of importance. (Give a few examples.)
    Show Card 3
14. In your present job, could you say whether each of these items is good, average or poor? E.g. Would you say that your pay was good, average or poor, etc?
15. Which on the list would you say was best catered for in your job?
16. Which on the list would you say was the worst catered for in your job?
    Remove Card 2
17. Which of the statements on this card come closest to describing how you feel about your job?
    Show Card 4
18. Is there anything about your job that gives you a feeling of accomplishment or achievement?
19. Is there anything about your job that makes you feel particularly irritable or frustrated?
20. Do you think your job is essential to the success of Gourmets?
21. If you had the chance to move to another job in Gourmets, would you do so?
    Why is that?
22. Do you understand how your pay is calculated in your present job?
    If Yes How is it calculated?
            How did you get to know this?
    If No Has anyone explained the new system to you?
            If Yes Who explained it to you?
23. Do you prefer the present pay system to the old one?
    Why is that?
24. How friendly would you say you are with the people who work near you?
    Show Card 5
25. Is there anyone in your department who you would regard as a particular friend?
26. How often would you say you talked with the people who work with you?
    Show Card 6
27. Where do you usually eat your meals?

Canteen
Other

163

28. With whom do you usually eat your meals?
29. How would you feel if you were forced to move from your present job to a similar one (in the region)?
    Show Card 7
    Why is this?
30. Have you ever applied to be a supervisor?
    If Yes What happened?
    If No Is there any reason why you haven't done so?
31. Are you (still) interested in becoming a supervisor?
32. What do you think is the most attractive thing offered by being a supervisor?
33. What do you think is the least attractive thing offered by being a supervisor?
34. Do you think that the right people are chosen as supervisors?
35. How would you say your supervisor compared with other supervisors in the firm?
    Show Card 1
36. How friendly would you say that you are with your supervisor?
    Show Card 5
37. What do you think of the training offered by Gourmets to new employees?
38. What do you think of the welfare schemes offered by Gourmets to its employees?

SECTION 3. THE REPRESENTATIVE SYSTEM

I should now like to ask you a few questions on the trade union and works' committee systems at Gourmets. I stress again that your answers will be treated with the strictest confidence.

39. Are you a member of a trade union?

If No to Question 39

40. Is there any reason why you are not a member of a trade union?
41. Have you ever been a member of a trade union branch?
    If Yes Which branch was that?
        If Gourmets Why did you leave?

If Yes to Question 39

42. How did you come to join?
43. Have you ever held any office in the branch?
    If Yes What office was that?
        Can you tell me how you came to hold that office?
        Can you tell me why you came to give it up?
    If No Would you be interested in holding office?
        Why is this?

44. When did you last attend a branch meeting?
45. About how many branch meetings have you attended in the past twelve months?
46. About what proportion of the total was this?

All
Over half
About half
Less than half
None

47. Did you vote in the last branch election?
48. Would you like to be a full-time union official?
    Why is this?

All trade union members and non-members
49. Who is your shop-steward?
50. How often do you see him/her on union business?
    Show Card 8
51. How friendly would you say you are with your shop-steward?
    Show Card 5
52. Do you think that everyone should be a member of a trade union?
    Why do you say this?
53. What do you think are the main advantages and satisfactions to be gained from being a shop-steward?
54. What do you think are the main disadvantages and dissatisfactions suffered by shop-stewards?
55. Are you a departmental committee or works' committee member?
    If Yes Which office?
             Could you tell me how you came to hold this office?
    If No Have you ever stood for election as a committee member?
        If Yes What happened?
                 Are you still interested in becoming a member?
        If No Have you ever considered standing?
                 Will you stand in the future?

Unless departmental representative
56. Who is your departmental representative?
57. How often do you see him on committee business?
    Show Card 8
58. How friendly would you say you are with him?
    Show Card 5

Unless works' committee representative
59. Who is your works' committee representative?

165

60. How often do you see him on committee business?
    Show Card 8
61. How friendly would you say you are with him?
    Show Card 5
62. How important a role do you think the departmental committees and works' committees play in Gourmets?
    Show Card 3
63. How would you feel if the committees had to be done away with?
    Show Card 7
64. When you have a complaint, how often would you say you took it up?
    Show Card 6
65. When you take up a grievance, to whom do you first report it?

    Foreman
    Chargehand
    Shop-steward
    Manager
    Other

66. How often would you say that you had cause for complaint?
    Show Card 8
67. How would you feel if the trade union was unable to continue at Gourmets?
    Show Card 7

SECTION 4

I shall now read to you a series of statements which will relate to management, union and supervisors. I would like you to tell me whether or not you agree with each of these statements.

68. The management at Gourmets are genuinely interested in the well being of the workers.
69. Managers have an extremely interesting job.
70. The managers at Gourmets are paid too much.
71. The managers at Gourmets would put one over on the workers if they had a chance.
72. Managers have a more difficult job than many people think.
73. Higher management are more able to look after the best interests of the workers than trade union officials.
74. The higher management at Gourmets are out of touch with the feelings of the workers.
75. Most supervisors at Gourmets have not got enough authority.
76. Gourmets could run just as well without supervisors.
77. Supervisors at Gourmets are paid too much.

78. Most supervisors at Gourmets are concerned about the welfare of the workers in their departments.
79. Full-time trade union officials understand the feelings of the workers on the shop floor.
80. Most trade unions are run by a small clique who are out for themselves.
81. Rank and file members of a union should only trouble the shop-stewards when they have a grievance to settle.
82. Gourmets could run just as well without the shop-stewards.

SECTION 5. COMMUNITY PARTICIPATION

This is the last section, and in it I should like to ask you a few questions about your family, and the things that you do in your leisure time.
83. Are you married?
    If Yes a. What job does your wife/husband do?
            b. Have you any children?
            If Yes i. How many?
                  ii. How old are they?
                  iii. What jobs do they do?
84. Which school did you last attend?
          School
          Type
          Age of leaving
85. Since you left school, have you been on any full-time or part-time courses?
    Type of course   Dates
86. If you were 15 again today, would you take up the same occupation?
87. What advice would you give a boy/girl aged 15 today, who is thinking about leaving school and taking a job?
88. Are there any clubs or societies, or other local organisations, or local branches of national organisations of which you are a member?
How do the people that you meet there feel about Gourmets?
How do they feel about the union?
89. Are there any things that you think I should have asked you about in this survey, that I have left out?
90. Have you any questions that you would like to ask me?

CARDS

Cards, with contents as shown below, were handed to respondents at the points indicated in the schedule.

Card 1
1. The best
2. One of the best
3. Average
4. One of the worst
5. The worst

Card 2
1. The work not too difficult
2. Easy to get to
3. Good pay
4. Good working conditions
5. Convenient hours
6. Friendly workmates
7. Understanding supervisors
8. Good social facilities
9. Security of employment
10. Good chance of promotion
11. Chance to do something worthwhile
12. Strong trade union branch
13. Good shop-stewards

Card 3
1. An absolute must
2. Very important
3. Quite important
4. Not really important
5. Not important at all

Card 4
1. Interesting nearly all the time
2. Interesting most of the time — some dull stretches
3. Interesting some of time — mostly dull and monotonous
4. Completely dull and monotonous

Card 5
1. Extremely friendly
2. Quite friendly
3. Indifferent
4. Not very friendly
5. Don't know each other

Card 6
1. Almost always
2. More than half the time
3. About half the time
4. Less than half the time
5. Almost never

Card 7
1. Very badly
2. Quite badly
3. Wouldn't mind all that much
4. Wouldn't mind at all
5. Be pleased

Card 8
1. At least once a day
2. Once a week
3. Once a month
4. Less than once a month
5. Almost never

References

W. Baldamus, *Efficiency and Effort: An Analysis of Industrial Administration*, Tavistock, London, 1961.

J. A. Banks, *Industrial Participation, Theory and Practice: A Case Study*, Liverpool University Press, Liverpool, 1963.

P. A. Baran and P. M. Sweezy, *Monopoly Capital*, Penguin Books, London, 1968.

L. Baritz, *The Servants of Power*, Wiley, Science Editions, New York, 1965.

H. Behrend, 'The Effort Bargain', *Industrial and Labour Relations Review*, vol. 10, no. 4 (July 1957).

D. Bell, *The End of Ideology*, The Free Press, Glencoe, Ill., 1960.

P. L. Van den Berghe, *Race and Racism. A Comparative Perspective*, J. Wiley and Sons, New York, 1967.

R. M. Blackburn, *Union Character and Social Class*, B. T. Batsford, London, 1967.

R. Blauner, *Alienation and Freedom: The Factory Worker and his Industry*, University of Chicago Press, Chicago, 1964.

P. Blumberg, *Industrial Democracy: The Sociology of Participation*, Constable, London, 1968.

R. K. Brown, 'Participation, Conflict and Change in Industry. A review of research in industrial sociology at the Department of Social Science, University of Liverpool', *The Sociological Review*, vol. 13, no. 3 (Nov. 1965).

'Research and Consultancy in Industrial Enterprises. A review of the contribution of the Tavistock Institute of Human Relations to the development of industrial sociology', *Sociology*, vol. 1, no. 1 (Jan. 1967).

J. Child, *British Management Thought: A Critical Analysis*, Allen and Unwin, London, 1969.

E. Chinoy, *Automobile Workers and the American Dream*, Doubleday, New York, 1955.

H. A. Clegg, A. J. Killick and R. Adams, *Trade Union Officers*, Blackwell, Oxford, 1961.

S. Cunnison, *Wages and Work Allocation*, Tavistock, London, 1966.

S. Dassa, 'L'analyse contextuelle appliquée aux orientations et aux comportements syndicaux', *Sociologie du Travail*, vol. 10, no. 4 (Oct.-Dec. 1968).

I. Deutscher, 'Words and Deeds: Social Science and Social Policy', *Social Problems,* vol. 13, no. 3 (Winter 1966).

N. T. Dodge, *Women in the Soviet Economy: Their Role in Economic, Scientific and Technical Development,* The Johns Hopkins Press, Baltimore, 1966.

A. Etzioni, *A Comparative Analysis of Complex Organisations,* The Free Press, Glencoe, Ill., 1961.

F. E. Fielder, 'A Note on Leadership Theory: The Effect of Social Barriers Between Leaders and Followers', *Sociometry,* vol. 20, no. 2 (June 1957).

E. Gellner, 'Concepts and Society', in D. Emmet and A. MacIntyre (eds.), *Sociological Theory and Philosophical Analysis,* Macmillan, London, 1970.

R. L. Gold, 'Roles in Sociological Field Observations', *Social Forces,* vol. 36, no. 3 (March 1958).

J. H. Goldthorpe, D. Lockwood, E. Bechhofer and J. Platt, *The Affluent Worker: Industrial Attitudes and Behaviour,* Cambridge University Press, Cambridge, 1968.

The Affluent Worker in the Class Structure, Cambridge University Press, Cambridge, 1969.

A. W. Gouldner, *Patterns of Industrial Bureaucracy,* The Free Press, Glencoe, Ill., 1954.

'Organisational Analysis', in R. K. Merton, L. Broom, L. S. Cottrell Jr. (eds.), *Sociology Today: Problems and Prospects,* vol. II, Harper and Row, New York, 1959.

'The Unemployed Self', in Ronald Fraser (ed.), *Work 2,* Penguin Books, London, 1969.

H.M.S.O., *Ministry of Labour Gazette,* vol. LXXV (Jan. 1967).

Social Trends, no. 1, 1970.

E. C. Hughes, 'The Sociological Study of Work: An Editorial Foreword', *American Journal of Sociology,* vol. 57, no. 5 (March 1952).

C. L. Hulin and P. C. Smith, 'Sex Differences in Job Satisfaction', *Journal of Applied Psychology,* vol. 48, no. 2 (April 1964).

A. Hunt, *A Survey of Women's Employment,* Government Social Survey, H.M.S.O., London, 1968.

G. K. Ingham, *Size of Industrial Organization and Worker Behaviour,* Cambridge University Press, Cambridge, 1970.

International Labour Office, *Women Workers in a Changing World,* Report VI (1), International Labour Conference, 48th Session, 1963, I.L.O., Geneva, 1964.

P. Jephcott, N. Seear and J. H. Smith, *Married Women Working,* Allen and Unwin, London, 1962.

V. Klein, *Britain's Married Women Workers*, Routledge and Kegan Paul, London, 1965.

J. Kolaja, *A Polish Factory: A Case Study of Workers' Participation in Decision Making*, University of Kentucky Press, Lexington, 1960.

A. Kornhauser, *Mental Health of the Industrial Worker*, John Wiley and Sons, New York, 1965.

S. M. Lipset, M. A. Trow and J. S. Coleman, *Union Democracy: The internal politics of the International Typographical Union*, The Free Press, Glencoe, Ill., 1956.

Liverpool University Department of Social Science, *The Dockworker*, Liverpool University Press, Liverpool, 1954.

T. Lupton, *On the Shop Floor*, Pergamon Press, London, 1963.

W. E. J. McCarthy and S. R. Parker, Royal Commission on Trade Unions and Employers' Associations, Research Paper 10, *Shop Stewards and Workshop Relations*, H.M.S.O., London, 1968.

R. Marriot, *Incentive Payment Schemes: A Review of Research and Opinion*, Staples, London, 1961.

K. Marx, *The Eighteenth Brumaire of Louis Bonaparte*, Progress Publishers, Moscow, 1954.

S. M. Peck, *The Rank-and-File Leader*, College and University Press, New Haven, 1963.

C. G. Renold, *Joint Consultation over 30 years*, Allen and Unwin, London, 1950.

D. F. Roy, 'Work Satisfaction and Social Reward in Quota Achievement: An Analysis of Piecework Incentive', *American Sociological Review*, vol. 28, no. 5 (Oct. 1953).

'Efficiency and "The Fix": Informal Intergroup Relations in a Piecework Machine Shop', *American Journal of Sociology*, vol. 60, no. 3 (Nov. 1954).

'The Union-Organising Campaign as a Problem of Social Distance: Three Crucial Dimensions of Affiliation – Disaffiliation', in H. S. Becker, B. Geer, D. Riesman and R. S. Weiss (eds.), *Institutions and the Person: Papers Presented to Everett C. Hughes*, Aldine, Chicago, 1968.

L. R. Sayles, *Behaviour of Industrial Work Groups: Prediction and Control*, J. Wiley and Sons, New York, 1958.

W. H. Scott, E. Mumford, I. C. McGivering and J. M. Kirby, *Coal and Conflict: A study of Industrial Relations at the Collieries*, Liverpool University Press, Liverpool, 1963.

W. I. Thomas, *The Unadjusted Girl*, Harper Torchbook, New York, 1967.

W. I. and D. S. Thomas, *The Child in America*, Alfred A. Knopf, New York, 1928.

171

C. R. Walker and R. H. Guest, *The Man on the Assembly Line,* Harvard
   University Press, Cambridge, 1952.
W. F. Whyte, *Street Corner Society: The Social Structure of an Italian Slum,*
   Chicago University Press, Chicago, 1955.
J. Woodward, *Industrial Organization: Theory and Practice,* Oxford
   University Press, London, 1965.
   'Automation and Technical Change: The Implication for the Management
   Process', in O.E.C.D., *Manpower Aspects of Automation and Technical
   Change,* Supplement to Final Report, European Conference, Zurich,
   Feb. 1966.

Index

Absenteeism 11, 15
Achievement, sense of 53, 73, 75, 78, 85, 154, 163
Action approach 3, 153, 157-8
Actor 156
Adjustment
  to factory work 41, 59
  to limited rewards attainable 6, 24, 153, 158-9
Advertising for supervisor 96-7
Age 2, 9, 21, 24, 25-7, 33, 36-8, 39, 48, 61, 92, 144, 152-3, 155
  related to job 26-7, 32, 116, 160n
Alienation 5, 144, 147
Apathetic work group behaviour 153, 155
Atmosphere on shop floor 46-51, 60, 63, 71, 81 and see friends
Attitudes of workers 5, 19, 156-8, 161, and see work, etc.
Automobile workers 2n, 4-5, 77, 78, 90
Autonomy 18, 35, 38, 93

Baldamus, W. 82n
Bank clerks 117n
Banks, J. A. 88n, 137n
Baran, P. A. 13n
Bargaining, collective see negotiation
Baritz, L. 144n
Behaviour of workers 2-6, 71, 112, 153-8, 160
Behrend, H. 82n
Bell, D. 16n
Belt workers 16, 17-18, 20, 21, 26-8, 30, 34, 36, 51, 72-3, 84, 112-13, 129, 155
  auxiliary 17-18, 20, 22, 37-8, 53, 78, 113, 154
  direct 17-18, 22, 53, 77, 156
Van den Berghe 23
Belts, conveyor 16, 18, 77-8, 85, 153-4, 156
'Better job', desire for 53, 76, 92, 150, 152, 155
Blackburn, R. M. 117n, 119n
Blauner, R. 52n, 78n, 86n, 153n
Blumberg, P. 144n
Boring work 75-7, 87, 149, 158-9

Breadwinner 63, 64
Breakdown, mechanical 77-8, 83-4, 85
  social 77-8
Brown, R. K. 2n
Building industry 41

Cadbury 13
Canteen 7, 82, 121, 129, 163
  workers 72
Car workers see automobile workers
Case study 6-7, 155n
Changes desired 52
Child, J. 13n
Children 6, 24-5, 28, 36, 81, 92, 148n, 152, 167
  dependent 4, 9, 29-31, 32, 36, 84, 86, 147
  independent 25, 28-9, 33, 147
Chinoy, E. 78, 90
Choice of firm 39, 41-5, 59, 113, 146, 162
Choice of job 3-5, 37, 143, 157, 160-1
  opportunity for 160
Class, social 2, 5, 144
  consciousness 143
  history and tradition 117
  inequality 144
  shared experience 15, 23-4, 33
  working 14, 96, 144-5, 146, 148
Cleaners 18-19, 20, 25-6, 38, 72, 78
Cleaning, office 21
  part-time 148
  school 40
Clegg, H. A. 107n
Clerical work 31, 36, 40, 44, 119-20, 159
Clock number 9
Clocking in, out 15, 51
Collective action 5, 113, 133, 140, 141, 149, 153, 156
  organisation 5, 112
  orientation 149
  solidarity 37, 118, 142, 143, 161
Community 24
Comparative analysis 6, 144
Compliance 6, 102
Conditions of service 7, 53-4, 146
Conditions, working 46-8, 50-1, 59, 61-6, 70, 79, 84, 130-1

Conflict, industrial 11, 13, 14, 115, 143
  of interests 2, 35, 37
  with management 112, 134
  between shop stewards and workers
    134-6
  with supervision 78
  at work 77-8, 83-4, 90, 100, 108,
    140-1, 143
  within work group 124, 143
Congruence of expectations and rewards
  67-72, 84, 86, 157
Conservative work group 153
Consistency of attitudes 158n
Consultation 2, 13
Consultation, joint 14, 88, 107, 136-40,
    141, 146
  attitudes to 108, 139-40
  committee members 137-8, 165;
    relations with workers 137-8, 165-6
  committees 107, 138, 141; ex-members
    of 137
  ideology of 107n
  importance of 138-40, 141
  influence of 138, 140
  interest in standing for office 137-8
  knowledge of system 138-40, 165-6
  participation in 138
Contextual effect 120, 124n, 127n, and
  see social context
Control by management 37, 64, 71, 78,
    93, 101-2
  by workers 2, 5, 82-3, 86-7, 90, 114,
    150, 161
Control system 51, 55, 56, 65, 82-4, 88,
    100-1, 105-6, 114, 149-52
Conway Stewart 146
Creativity in a job 5
Culture 156
Cunnison, S. 145n

Dassa, S. 124n, 127n
Definition of situation 3, 7, 160
Depressed area 13
Depression, the 24
Deprivations at work 159
Deutscher, I. 8n
Discrimination against women 146
Dispute see conflict
Dissatisfaction 49, 55, 60, 63, 65, 71, 72,
    76, 85-6, 90, 97, 101, 106, 112,
    144, 149, 151, 154, 159
Division of labour 15, 17, 21, 23, 24
Divisions within the workforce 15, 22, 33,
    34, 144

working class 144
Dodge, N. T. 148n

Easy to get to work see nearness to home
Easy work 61-6, 71
  for shop stewards 132
  for supervisors 92-3
Ecological fallacy 161n
Economic coercion 77, 151, 155
  incentive 152
  necessity 36, 59, 64, 86-7, 92, 147,
    149
  rewards see rewards
'Effort bargain' 82
'Ego satisfaction' 91-3, 132
Employment situation 42, 45, 48-9, 86,
    90, 111, 144, 146, 156
Endlessly the same, work 76-7
Erratic work group behaviour 153, 155
Ethnic origin 2
Ethnocenticity 14
'Ethos' of firm 46-7
Etzioni, A. 86n
Evaluations of firm see firm, assessment of
Expectations from supervisors 71, 96, 100,
    104, 105-6
  from work 1, 3, 6, 23, 24, 35, 49, 60,
    61-72, 84-7, 99, 105, 112, 148-52,
    155, 157-60, and see utopian
    expectations
Experience of work, nature of 1, 4, 56, 86,
    93, 106, 122-3, 149, 151, 152,
    157-9
Exploitation of women 147

Factory records clerks 18-19, 72, 75
Factory work 159
  availability of 21
  experience of 40, 59, 119, 148-9
Family 28-31, 150
  centred 81, 85, 146, 150-1
  factors 104
  problems 55, 58
  responsibilities 9, 28, 33, 36-7, 42, 44,
    48-9, 60, 63-4, 81, 84, 104, 148-50,
    152, 160; related to job 30-1
  roles 4, 58, 60, 81, 86, 147-8, 152, 159
  situation 5-6, 16, 24-5, 27-31, 33, 35-8,
    40, 144, 146, 148-50, 167; related
    to age 28-9
Family firm 13, 55-6, 59, 162
Fielder, F. E. 101n
Firm, assessment of 42, 45-55, 56, 59-60,
    87, 148-50, 162

attractions 46-9
disadvantages 49-52
Firm, market situation of 13, 146
Folklore of the factory 52, 83
Freedom of movement 18, 38, 72, 154
Friends at work 24, 46-8, 51, 54, 59-60,
   63-6, 80-2, 84, 86, 92, 100, 147-8,
   159, 161, 163, *and see* workmates
   close 80-1, 85, 99, 149, 151
   loss of in supervisory job 89, 93-4
   opportunity to make 81
   particular 80-1, 163
   as reason for choosing firm 43-5
   as reason for not leaving firm 54
   as reason for not changing job 80, 85,
     147, 149
   talking to 45, 73, 85, 101
   with committee representative 138,
     164
   with supervisor 98-100, 106, 164
Fringe benefits 39, 48, 59, 92, 146, 150
Frustration 73, 74-8, 85-6, 154-5, 163

Gellner, E. 158n
Gold, R. L. 8n
Goldthorpe, J. H. 3n, 4, 5, 131n, 158-9
Gouldner, A. W. 3-4, 100n
Grievance procedure 108, 111
Grievances 107-13, 130, 156
   acted on 109-12, 133, 140-1, 151, 166
   frequency of 108-12, 141, 149, 151,
     166
Guest, R. H. 2n, 78n

Holidays 76
Hours of work 15, 42, 44, 46-8, 51, 60,
   71, 104
   convenience for home life 44-5, 58,
     59-60, 61-6, 68, 70, 84, 148, 150
   government regulation of 16, 23
Housewife 40, 44, 119, 147
Housing 13
Hulin, C. L. 145n
Human Relations 1-2, 5, 13, 101, 144
Hunt, A. 144n, 148n

'Ideal' jobs 76
Identity, social 86, 146, 150
Image of firm 45, 146
Importance of job 53, 64
   of trade-unionism 113, 114
   of work 86, 147
Important aspects of job 60, 61-3, 64,
   67-72, 82, 84, 86, 100, 106,
   148-52, 155, 157, 162

Industrial sociology 1, 144-5, 153, 157-9
Informality on night shift 9, 94, 99-101,
   104, 106, 150, 152
Ingham, G. K. 11n
Inspectors 18-19, 20, 72, 75, 154
Instrumental involvement in firm 55, 60,
   99, 106
   involvement in work 104, 150, 155
   orientation 4, 5, 74, 88, 135, 151-2,
     157, 159
   satisfaction 152
Interesting work 54, 72-3, 76, 79, 84,
   85-6, 132, 136, 151, 154-5, 157
   lack of 72, 74, 79, 85, 154, 159
I.L.O. 145n
Interviewing 8-9
Intrinsic satisfaction 75, 85, 86, 93, 149,
   154-5
   rewards *see* rewards
Involvement 1, 3, 11, 86, 104, 105, 114,
   144, 152, 157, *and see* instrumental
   in firm 2-3, 13, 39, 53-5, 59-60, 86-7,
     88, 92, 99, 104, 120, 152
   in job 84-7, 92, 94, 149-52
   in union *see* union *and* unionism
   in work 30, 58, 60, 63, 64, 67-8, 85-7,
     96, 99, 106, 112, 113, 116, 122,
     138, 141, 146-50, 152, 159
Isolation, social, of individual 9, 91, 98,
   112-13, 130, 134, 142
   of miners 100n
   of night shift 36-7, 97, 99, 101, 104,
     115-16, 138, 142

Jephcott, P. 145n
Job 1, 61, 104, 160, 162-3
   attitudes to 72-9, 154
   availability of 4, 145, 147, 160
   desire to change 79-80, 92
   evaluations of 63-72, 84, 161, 163;
     attractions 64-72; disadvantages
     65-72
   role 5, 51, 53, 55, 60, 71, 72-80, 100,
     106, 164
   types of 16, 17-19, 151
Journey to work 31, 42, *and see* nearness
   to home

Klein, V. 145n
Kolaja, J. 8n
Kornhauser, A. 152n

Labour exchange 42
Labour market 1, 3, 36, 152
   experience of 4, 39

local 1, 145
    position in 44, 46, 87, 145-6
Labour relations, 'enlightened' 107
Labour turnover 11, 14, 81, 147, 148n
lateness 15
latent roles 2, 5
'latent social identities' 3
leisure facilities 13, 48-9, 59-60, 61-3, 71,
    84, 146
length of service 24, 31-3, 34, 37-8, 39,
    81, 89-90, 105, 162
life cycle 24-5, 28-9, 35, 149
'life-cycle squeeze' 61
Lipset, S. M. 6n, 81n
Liverpool University, Department of
    Social Science 2, 56n
Loneliness at home 44, 59-60, 147
Lupton, T. 145n

McCarthy, W. E. J. 107n
Maintenance staff 78
Management 1, 9, 158, 160
    interest in workers 55, 57, 59, 166
    out of touch with workers 56-7, 166
    policies 13, 23, 55, 146
    power 4, 161
    professional 14
    'putting one over' 57-8, 59, 83, 166
    rewards of 5, 56-7, 166
    structure 2, 15
    theory 14
    workers' attitudes to 46, 55-9
    workers' relations with 59
Manufacturing process 15-16, 77, and see
    technology of production
Married women, husbands' attitudes to
    working 44-5
    opportunity to work 44, 59-60, 147-8
    reasons for working 3, 44, 92, 147
    return to work 44-5, 147
Marriott, R. 82n
Marx, K. 114n
Mass production see technology of
    production
Meaning of work 3, 33, 146, 161
Men's work 21-3, 37-8, 113, 145-6
Militancy 33
    of shop stewards 107n
Monotonous work 72, 75-6, 78, 112, 154,
    and see boring work and interest,
    lack of

Nearness to home 24, 42-5, 48-9, 59, 64-6,
    71, 84, 148

Negotiation 22, 106, 107, 129, 136
    machinery 88
Nepotism 89-90
News of the World 146
Night allowance see pay
Non-work life 3, 4, 23, 81, 135, 145-6,
    152, 167
    factors 4, 157-8, 161

Observational research 7-8
Operator 17, 21, 28, 30, 32, 34, 36
    machine 17-18, 20, 22, 26, 154
    process 16, 17-18, 20, 37, 38, 142, 154
Organisational structure of firm 1, 3, 5, 33
Orientations to union 114, 119, 141
Orientations to work 3-6, 9, 36, 38, 48,
    84, 101, 112, 114, 140-1, 155-61,
    and see instrumental
    dominant aspect 5, 158, 159
    in relation to work situation 7, 158-9,
    161
Ownership 13, 55

Pace of work 16, 72, 77, 154
    machine set 18
Packaging and wrapping 16, 18, 21-3, 30,
    36, 37, 77, 112, 154, 156
Parker, S. R. 107n
Participation 2
Paternalism 13, 14, 148
Pay 19-21, 35, 39, 42-5, 46-8, 53-4, 59-60,
    61-6, 70-1, 76, 79, 84, 92, 104, 130,
    148-50, 152, 157, and see rewards,
    economic
    grades 20, 22
    incentive 15, 18, 19, 72, 82
    level of 15, 37, 43, 45, 51, 82-3, 84,
    146, 147, and see wage rates
    loss of 78
    night allowance 20, 22, 145, 150
    in previous jobs 104
    women's rates 15, 21, 145
Payment system 14, 15, 19, 52, 82-4, 85,
    90, 146, 163
    ignorance of how pay calculated 19,
    52, 82-3
    ignorance of change of system 83
    new system 52, 83, 84, 120-1
    old system 52, 83
Peck, S. M. 128n
Pensions 48, 60, 150
Permanent job, lack of 17-18, 21, 27, 36,
    51, 77, 81, 95

Personnel departments for men and women 23
  manager 80, 107n
  policies 146
Political skills 134
Power relationships 15, 23, *and see* management power
Powerlessness 78
Previous employment 31, 36, 39-40, 104
Printers 81n
Privatised workers 4, 158
Production process 15-16, 21, 35, 61, 72, 82, 150, *and see* technology of production
Promotion 32
  desire for 22, 79, 88, 91
  to present job 19, 30
  prospects 22, 37, 61-6, 71-2, 84-5, 89
  system 71, 88-90, 94, 96, 105, 152

Quota, completion of 73, 78, 154

Radio Caroline 85, 101
Recruitment of employees 22, 37
  to union *see* union
Relatives in the firm 24
Religion 2
Renold, C. G. 107n
Repression of feelings of frustration 74, 78
Responsibility 27, 72, 88, 157
Restriction of output 82n, 116n
Retail work 21, 39-40, 44, 119-20, 148, 159
Retirement 25, 48, 55
Rewards of the job 15, 61, 63-72, 157, 161
  economic 5, 42, 48-51, 55, 59-60, 61, 64, 83, 92, 104, 150, 152
  evaluations of 4, 65-72, 84, 86
  extrinsic 152-3
  intrinsic 150-1
  limited range possible 4, 24, 153, 158-9, *and see* adjustment
  non-economic 158-9
  social 49, 59-60, 104, 112, 147, 149, 151, 155
Rowntree 13
Roy, D. 73, 82n, 115
Royal Commission on Trade Unions and Employers Associations 107n
Rules 7, 9, 14, 15, 51, 78, 102, 149, 156

Sack, the 148
Sample 9-12

Satisfaction 2, 5, 18, 46, 49, 55, 63-72, 73, 80, 85-7, 111, 144, 145, 148-52, 153-5, 159, *and see* instrumental *and* intrinsic
  with firm 52, 53, 60
Sayles, L. R. 153, 155
School leavers 39, 40, 119-20
  choice of first job 3, 43
  in first job 39, 104, 112, 149
  girl 5-6
School meals service 40, 148
Scientific management 1-2
Scott, W. H. 11n
Screaming 75-6
Sex 2, 21, 24, 33, 144-5, 160
  roles in wider society 35, 84, 152, 159, *and see* family
Security 39, 42, 48, 55, 59-60, 61-6, 68, 70-1, 84, 87, 104, 147, 149-50, 152
  of husband 63, 147
  of supervisors 92
'Self' of worker 4, 5, 6
Self-fulfilling prophecy 117
Shop stewards 7, 9, 10, 14, 19, 22, 83, 107, 114, 116, 119, 128-36, 158, 165
  ability to do job of 134
  attitudes to 133-6
  criticism of 132-5, 141-2
  interest in becoming 133, 135-6, 164
  job of 37, 131-6, 164
  on joint consultative committees 137-8
  length of service 34, 129
  marginality 134
  relations with 129-36, 138, 142-3, 155, 164
  senior 115-16, 129, 136, 137n
  women 114n, 116-17, 137, 142-3
Shop-stewards' committee 7, 136, 150
Size of department 10, 22, 97-8, 138
Skill 16, 32, 145
Smith, P. C. 145n
Smoking, rule forbidding 51, 78
Social characteristics 1, 15, 16, 23-33, 35, 145, 146, 157, 161
Social context 5, 21, 23, 33, 35, 120, 161, *and see* contextual effect
Social facilities *see* leisure facilities
Social factors 6, 51, 147
Social pressures to join union 119, 124, 133, 142
Social relationships 2, 6, 35, 39, 51, 61, 77, 79, 135, 145, 149, 151-2, 153, 155-6, 161
Social rewards *see* rewards

Social structure *see* work situation, structure of
Social Trends 144n, 148n
Socialisation in the job 24, 158
Status in community 146, 150
  compared with 'ego satisfaction' 91-2, 132
  of job 19, 37, 78-9, 90, 91-2, 154·
  of shop steward 135
Strategic work group behaviour 153, 156
Strike 33, 84, 115-16, 120-1, 156
  meeting 116, 121
Structural pluralism 23
Students 115-16, 156
Style of life 150
Subculture 23, 35, 37, 99-100, 106
Supervision 88-106, 150, 152, 160
  style of leadership 2, 101
Supervisor, job of 88-94, 102-3
  ability to do 89-90, 96-7, 105
  advantages and disadvantages 90-4, 164
  application for 88-9, 105, 164
  desire for 88-9, 92, 164
  marginality 93
  necessity of 102-3, 166
  performance of 92-4
  responsibility of 88, 93
  workers' views of 89-94, 164
Supervisors 7, 9, 63-6, 78, 82, 94-105
  ability of 96-7, 105
  age in relation to age of workers 51-2, 96-7, 99, 101, 149
  attitudes to 79, 91-2, 102-5
  authority of 104-5, 166
  concern for workers' well-being 103-5, 106
  criticism of 51-2, 56, 60, 91-3, 94-7, 100, 105, 128, 132-3, 149
  pay 102-3, 166
  relations with 71, 78, 85, 88, 91, 93-101, 104, 105-6, 155
  'sticking up for girls' 96, 100-1, 104 105, 143
  worker's own 97-102, 104, 165-6
Sweezy, P. M. 13n

Tavistock Institute 2
Technological implications approach 2, 37, 153, 154, 157, 159
Technology 153-6
  influence of 2, 4, 10, 51, 72, 112, 153-6
Technology of production
  craft 153

mass production 16, 60, 72, 77, 85, 153-4, 156
process (flow) 16, 17, 22, 153
Technology of work situation 2, 3, 5-7, 10, 16, 51, 72, 112, 154-5, 157
Thomas, D. S. 3n
Thomas, W. I. 3n
Time spent at work 58, 75, 81, 85, 92, 96, 106, 150, 152, 155, *and see* hours
Time worker 17-19, 21, 26, 30-1, 34, 36, 72, 75, 78, 82, 160n
  manual 17-19, 38, 154, 160
  non-manual 17-19, 31, 36, 86n, 154, 160
Trade union *see* union
Tradition, Gourmet 13-14, 58, 107, 136, 141
Training for job 16, 32
Training scheme 41, 59, 107n, 164
Transport and General Workers Union 33
Trucking 22

Unemployment 6, 13, 39, 42-3, 45, 55, 59-60, 104, 150, 160
Union 6, 7, 33-4, 107, 113-28, 137, 146
  activist 115, 137n
  attitudes to 79, 108, 113-14, 141, 147
  availability of 119
  branch 33, 63-6, 113, 124-5, 129, 141-2, 156
  branch meetings 7, 108, 116, 164
  character 33
  collection of dues 107
  commitment to Brompton union 34, 124-8, 134, 141, 151
  criticism of 113, 120-2, 126-7, 128, 132, 134, 141-2
  development of 111, 115-17, 122, 133
  full-time official 107, 137n
  ideological support 117-19, 125, 128
  'men's affair' 115-17, 120, 128
  organisation 15, 34, 112, 114, 131
  relations with firm 33, 121, 126
  women and the union *see* women
  workers' relations with 71, 108, 115, 116, 122, 128
Union membership
  completeness 34, 37, 101, 107, 113-15, 120, 136
  ex-members 34, 37, 120, 122
  leaving 121-2, 164
  members 34, 115, 122-4, 127-8, 131, 133, 141-2, 144
  non-members 36, 37, 122-4, 127-8, 131, 133, 142

reasons for joining or not 117-22, 164; social 118-20
recruitment 34, 115, 136, 142-3; facilities for 14
Union shop 107, 115, 136
U.S.D.A.W. 119
U.S.S.R. 148n
Unionisation 9, 33, 37, 94, 97, 106, 113, 115, 142
Unionism
attitudes to 123, 142-3
'business' 117-18, 126
ideological commitment to 14, 116-18, 122-4, 128, 137n, 142-3
previous contact with 15, 119-20
status of, in factory 14
Utopian expectations 151, 152, 155, *and see* 'ideal' job

Values of workers 1, 89-90, 96
of owning family 55
Variables, explanatory 156, 160-1

Wage rates, in area 13, 20, 45, 59
comparable with Longborough 14
national average 20
Walker, G. R. 2n, 78n
Welfare schemes 13, 14
attitudes to 58, 60, 150, 164
knowledge of 58
Welfare State 14
Whyte, W. F. 7n
Women and support for the union 115-17, 120, 128, 130, 142-3, 149
Women workers, studies of 144-5
Women's work 21-3, 37, 52n, 113, 115, 145-6, 154
Woodward, Joan 2, 52n, 153
Worthwhile work *see* work
Work
as a central interest 36, 88, 115, 131

factors influencing workers 4, 35, 104, 156-7
nature of 15, 35, 51-2, 60, 64-6, 72, 75-6, 78, 85-6, 103, 106, 112, 141, 144, 149-50, 152, 154-6, *and see* technology
organisation of 33, 51-2, 60, 64, 85, 149-50
pleasant time at 150
role *see* job
routine 81
unrewarding 18, 72, 86, 104, 155; choice of 5
worthwhile 64-6, 71, 76, 84, 86, 152; not worthwhile 71, 75, 147
Work group
basis of involvement 120
composition 21, 67
influence 1
integration 2, 5, 153
norms 2, 5
solidarity 37, 113, 161
as source of satisfaction 80, 112
stable 51, 80-2, 85
as unit of study 160-1
Work situation 1, 2, 3, 6, 15, 33, 48, 51, 59, 71, 105, 112, 114, 138, 141-2, 145, 150-1, 156-8, 160-1
structure of 7, 33, 38, 77, 114, 145, 156, 159, 161
Workers, manual 5, 40, 48, 82n, 144, 146; unskilled 40, 119
non-manual 82n
'Working back' 2n
Workmates, relations with 49, 60, 85, 101, 155, *and see* friends
Works magazine 9

Young workers 20, 35-7, 60, 97, 152
men 16, 37, 48-9, 52, 59, 112, 134
women 6, 16, 75, 149

179